INDIANA'S FALSE HAUNTINGS

INDIANA'S FALSE HAUNTINGS

Stories of Pranks, Fakes and Supernatural Mistakes

ASHLEY M. WATSON, PHD

THE History PRESS

Published by The History Press
An imprint of Arcadia Publishing
Charleston, SC
www.historypress.com

First published 2025

Manufactured in the United States

ISBN 9781467158480
Hardcover ISBN 9781540299963

Library of Congress Control Number: 2025941133

To my father for giving me a love of history.

To my grandmother for giving me a love of ghosts.

CONTENTS

ACKNOWLEDGEMENTS

I want to thank my husband, James, and stepson, Hollis, for creating time and space for me to research and write this book. I also appreciate James's willingness to follow me and my ghost costume around Greater Lafayette, ultimately capturing great photos for the cover of the book. I also want to thank my father, mother, sister and brother for listening to me talk about ghosts each day of my life. Although they often sat on my drafts and tried to grab my pen, I am grateful for my cats Kitty Kitty Boo Boo and Wind for keeping me company during the long hours of writing. Finally, I want to thank the online Halloween Instagram community for supporting my research and offering words of encouragement.

Researching for this book solidified my ongoing appreciation for local historians, archivists and writers. Whether through online archives or written histories, their storytelling saved Hoosier histories from being lost and becoming inaccessible to a curious public. I specifically want to take time to thank the following: Indiana Memory online archives, Hoosier State Chronicles digital newspaper archives, Evansville author Joseph Engler, Evansville's Willard Library, Ruth Lilly Medical Library, Noble County Historical Society and Warren County historian Terri Wargo. Thank you for doing and sharing your work.

And finally, I want to thank John Rodrigue and Ryan Finn of The History Press and Arcadia Publishing for supporting local history and writers and for giving this ghost enthusiast a chance to share her spooky work.

INTRODUCTION

Ghost stories are [interesting] *even if there are no ghosts.*
—Rushville (IN) Republican, *May 20, 1938*

This is a book for believers and non-believers. This book will not answer the question: Do ghosts exists? And having an opinion one way or another is not required to enjoy this book. This is a book for people who have mistaken a pile of clothes on a bedroom chair as a nocturnal visitor. Or people who have jumped out of shadows to scare friends passing by. Or people woken up by the sounds of a ghostly pianist, only to find that it was their curious cat. The hauntings in this book—spoiler alert—turn out not to be ghosts. The unsolved mysteries outside this book? No comment.

This book archives newspaper stories of mistaken ghosts throughout the state of Indiana. Whether intentional pranks, unexpected animals or tricks of the mind, these published "ghost" stories turned out to be anything but. The stories—spanning from the late 1800s to the mid-1900s—speak to simpler times when neighborhood gossip of paranormal activity was worthy of print, especially if it was humorous or sensationalistic.

Ghosts in Print

Early in the nineteenth century and prior to the Civil War, newspapers had fewer pages and limited circulation, and the "content was dominated by politics and advocacy, reflecting their close ties to political parties and interest groups."[1] By the end of the century, several factors had changed American society, including industrialization, increased literacy, urbanization, an influx in immigration and technological and economic growth. This, in turn, brought proliferated growth in the production of newspapers. "The story of the growth of American newspapers," wrote David Sachsman in the introduction of *After the War: The Press in a Changing America, 1865–1900*, "is itself a story of industrial development based on large circulations, increasing advertising, and technological change."[2]

This resulted in the commercialization of the American newspaper and the rise of "New Journalism." During the 1870s, the total number of newspapers nearly doubled, many of which were dailies.[3] "This style of journalism," Sachsman wrote, "was all about news reporting that could even be called consumer reporting, since it was designed to provide readers with stories containing interesting and useful information for their everyday lives."[4] While politics still appeared in the press, it no longer solely determined the content. Now the business of newspapers "was in supplying readers to advertisers, rather than supporting a particular political ideology."[5]

Newspapers were now in the entertainment business, and this included the tried-and-true ghost story. In her chapter on ghost and crime news stories in *After the War*, Paulette D. Kilmer wrote, "Ghost stories blend daily existence with nightmares. They offer a neutral zone for confronting fear."[6] The following ghost stories are rather quotidian, to the point of asking: How was this news? Imaginative prose, along with ghosts being on the collective American mind, made these ghost stories entertaining and timely.

The Spiritualist movement, along with newspapers, also boomed after the Civil War as America dealt with its death toll and was seeking to communicate with those lost. Spiritualism in the nineteenth century was "a popular religious practice conducted through communication with the spirits of the dead."[7] The literature about the Spiritualist movement and its detractors is plentiful and includes many examples of fraudulent mediums. The innovative ways spiritualists materialized spirits (cheesecloth, animal parts, cracking joints and so on), while fascinating, open a larger debate on life after death that goes beyond the confines of the book. I, myself, an amateur scholar of Spiritualism, did not want to broach that subject without giving it the attention, grace and detail it deserves.

RESEARCH SITE AND METHODS

This project began when I entered the newspaper archives with the intention of finding ghost stories. What I found was a shocking number of non-ghost stories as well, which were often written with grandiose and dramatic flair. Eventually, I found myself with a pile of stories and a book project. Most of these newspapers are Indiana publications, although some news sources appear outside the state or the United States. Examples of out-of-state sources show how Hoosier ghost stories travel and entertain past state lines. The criteria were simple: there was a perceived haunting and there was a non-paranormal explanation, all taking place in Indiana and all notable enough to be published in the newspaper.

My research was limited to the late nineteenth and early twentieth centuries due to the popularity of local ghost stories in newspapers. Further, the endpoint was established prior to many technological innovations that opened a new frontier for mistaken paranormal activity and supernatural trickery. Further, mass media provided new ways to share ghost stories to a wider or more diverse audience (movies, television news and so on). As Kilmer once said in an interview, "[By] the time the 20th century comes around, ghost stories move into all kinds of different popular culture venues that don't exist in 1851."[8] I kept my endpoint to the 1950s and pre–*Amityville Horror*.

This book is as much about newspapers as it is about ghosts, so newspaper clippings were transcribed from sight as is. These ghost stories, Sachsman wrote, "were at the same time sensational and entertaining, and sometimes it was difficult to tell where the news ended and the reporters' imagination began."[9] I believe that summarizing these stories would not capture the reporters' imaginative talent.

Common themes revealed themselves during research: animals mistaken as ghosts, tricks of the mind causing confusion and pranksters and schemers acting as ghosts. A chapter is devoted to each theme and broken into further subcategories so to serve as a browseable reference book. The news clippings start with the location of the haunting followed by the news or archive source. Many of these stories are humorous or presented as so, but some are rather serious to the point of cautionary, especially in the final chapter. Pranks can result in injury to the prankster or the pranked. Readers will notice, for example, that guns were often used as protection against ghosts.

There are, of course, limitations in source material as with all archival work. Not all newspapers are digitalized, in readable condition, accessible to the public, dated and categorized correctly (due to human error) and so forth. Therefore, while this is a collection of ghost stories, it is by no means a complete or entirely comprehensive overview of this phenomenon. When available, multiple news articles are presented to provide fuller context to the ghost story—from mysterious sighting to debunking.

When necessary, brackets are used to fix distracting misspellings or provide contextual information. Since I was working with old documents, I had to make educated guesses, which also appear in brackets, of words that were difficult to decipher. Further, some paraphrasing was used with longer news clippings. Lastly, and important to note, some of the language used in these news articles is dated and problematic, and readers should go forth with a critical mind.

Writer Samuel Johnson once said of ghosts: "All argument is against it; but all belief is for it."[10] While this book is not an argument for or against ghosts, it heavily relies on the idea of belief. Belief is what materialized these Hoosier spirits into existence, and newspapers made them into legend.

Chapter 1

ANIMALS

Many a person who does not believe in ghosts is afraid of them.
—Daily Republican *(Rushville, IN), November 12, 1928*

The now defunct and demolished Riverside Amusement Park of Indianapolis sat on Thirtieth Street, east of the White River and next to the Riverside City Park.[11] The amusement park opened its gates to Indianapolis families in 1903 with free admission but with fees to participate in the attractions. The attractions were plentiful, including Shoot the Chutes, a miniature railway, the Old Mill boat ride, shooting galleries, Wavy Gee Whiz, a zoo with a black bear pit, the Thriller and Flash roller coasters, skating rinks, a dance pavilion, baseball diamonds and more at one time or another.[12]

While these attractions took some planning and building, other attractions appeared (super)naturally. On August 30, 1936, the *Indianapolis Sunday Star*[13] reported that the park's Haunted House was, well, *actually* haunted:

> *The "Haunted House" at Riverside amusement park has been really haunted! That has been the general opinion among park employes for the last two weeks. Deputy Sheriffs Taylor and Burleson, on special duty at the fun spot at nights, have been reporting strange shadows flitting about the parapet of the house after midnight and on several occasions have seen small green lights shining through the upper windows....*
>
> *The lights seemed to glow momentarily and then dim at intervals.*

Along with feline phantoms, visitors to the Riverside Amusement Park of Indianapolis could seek their thrills on the Thriller roller coaster. *Author's collection.*

Eventually, a park employee solved the haunting, which turned out to be more adorable than formidable:

> *A park employe was passing the haunted house, when out proudly marched Lizbeth, the park cat, who had been missing two weeks, followed by four baby kittens. It was discovered the blessed event had occurred in the cupola of the house, which is seldom visited. The strange shadows had been Lizbeth keeping a lookout over her brood as she prowled around the roof, and the strange green lights had been Lizbeth's eyes.*

With the mystery solved, deputies no longer avoided the house during their nightly rounds.

The park permanently closed in 1971, after sixty-eight years of existence, due to increasing repair costs, the suburban sprawl and racist admittance practices. The park leadership's refusal to remove "Patronage Whites Only Solicited" signs resulted in a mass protest by the local NAACP.[14] The park eventually opened its gates to all, but the damage was done. It seems that the legacy of the park was haunted by other means.[15]

Cats being mistaken as ghosts is not hard to imagine, as they are domesticated, ubiquitous and sly animals. Some of the animals causing hauntings are less predictable, though, as is the case with the haunted coffin on a New York Central train running through Elkhart, Indiana, in 1929.

Elkhart has an extensive transportation history, beginning in 1851 when Michigan Southern and Northern Indiana Railway (MS&NI) brought the first railway. Years later, MS&NI consolidated with Lake Shore Railroad, providing more connections.[16] The railroad increased population and, with the addition of a rail maintenance complex and other businesses, provided jobs for these citizens and would-be citizens. Then, by 1914, Lake Shore and Michigan Southern Railway had merged with the New York Central and Hudson River Railroad to become an enhanced New York Central.[17] Once termed the "Greatest Highway in the World," the New York Central Lines provided not only "fast and luxurious passenger trains" but also "rapid handling of freight."[18]

On May 23, 1929, the *Mitchell Tribune*[19] of Mitchell, Indiana, reported that freight on the train between Chicago and Cleveland (Train No. 28) had been mistaken for an otherworldly passenger:

> *When a New York Central express messenger heard rumbling grunts that appeared to come from a corpse in a coffin in the express car it was too much*

The New York Central Depot (named LS&MS Depot when the photo was taken) still stands and is located across from the National New York Central Railroad Museum in Elkhart, Indiana. *Author's collection.*

ghostly atmosphere for him. He [signaled] *frantically for the train to stop here* [Elkhart] *and leaped from the car even before the train had come to* [a full] *halt. As the express messenger fled from the scene he yelled out that he refused to ride any further with a "talking corpse."*

Two of the bravest remaining [trainmen] *investigated the cause of the express messenger's alarm. They boarded the express car. In the forward end was a coffin.*

They too, were startled to hear sounds almost like the mutterings that seemed to come from the direction of the corpse.

Investigating further, the trainmen discovered that the sounds came from a large box just in front of the coffin.

The box contained a shipment of live bull frogs.

The following news stories include more cats, birds, various farm animals, rodents, a bee colony and an out-of-place monkey. Whether a nocturnal piano solo (there are a few of those) or a reincarnated Christmas dinner, these stories are often written with dramatic flair and levity.

CATS

Shelbyville, Shelby County

Evansville (IN) Journal-News, May 20, 1916
CHAINS CLANK! GHOSTS? NO CAT IN STEEL TRAP
Residents in West Franklin street have been concerned with unusual noises…heard at all hours of the day and night. The sounds were similar to those made when a chain is dragged across a floor. Search was made by several persons, but not until yesterday was the cause determined. Mrs. John Fehr caught a cat, with one foot fastened in a steel trap, in her chicken house. The animal had been fastened in the trap for several days and had been dragging it in its travels about the neighborhood. When released, the injured foot fell off. The cat is being cared for by residents in the street.

Indianapolis, Marion County

Indianapolis (IN) News, September 21, 1896

Not Troubled by the Ghost Now

There is a new tenant on a farm northeast of the city where within a year a man murdered his wife and then hanged himself in the barn. The neighbors said a ghost had taken to walking there since the murder.

"I have killed the ghost," the new tenant said. "First he knocked down a stovepipe. I did not care much for this, but when the ghost began to frighten chickens to death and to tear them to pieces, I became interested. I loaded a shot-gun and lay in watching one night last week. Sure enough, there came the ghost. I fired point blank, and contrary to the result in other ghost stories, the victim fell; the shot had evidently gone through him and taken effect. You know usually a ghost is so airy that a bullet will not touch him. But I knocked my ghost out, and the shot were not charmed either. When I got to him the ghost was dead. There has been one fewer black cats in the neighborhood since, and I am missing no more chickens, and hearing no strange noises."

Richmond, Wayne County

Anderson (IN) Daily Bulletin, November 2, 1945

"Ghost" at Richmond Is Imprisoned Cat

A downtown funeral home was "haunted" for three days by a mysterious sound.

The source was found today. A cat had been "wrapped up" in a canvas chair container and returned along with some chairs that had been borrowed for a Halloween party.

Star City, Pulaski County

Anderson (IN) Herald, February 24, 1912

Cat Taken for Ghost

While Mrs. D.A. Skillen of Star City, was working in the kitchen yesterday, she was startled to hear the scale run on the piano in the parlor. Dr. Skillen was in the yard working on his automobile. She knew she was alone and the playing startled her. Presently a regular crescendo was executed and terror stricken, Mrs. Skillen rushed into the yard and excitedly told her husband a ghost was in the house playing the piano.

Dr. Skillen investigated and found the family cat running up and down the keyboard. Several times after the cat had to be chased from the piano. Dr. Skillen says that if the cat persists in playing he will get a regular piano teacher for him.

Anderson, Madison County

Morning Herald (Anderson, IN), March 4, 1897
PLAYED THE PIANO
A Cat Made a Neighborhood Look for a Ghost
Mr. and Mrs. John Amos live with her parents, Mr. and Mrs. Clem Chappell. A few nights ago Mr. and Mrs. Amos were alone in the house and the piano in another room began to sound. There was a run of the keys and a great noise for a few moments.

Mrs. Amos thought that in the jumbled discord a piece she often played was being repeated. With her husband she ran to the neighbors and a searching party was organized to find a ghost. It developed that the family cat had been amusing itself on the keyboard.

BIRDS

Monticello, White County

Monticello (IN) Herald, December 30, 1920
THE GHOST OF A GOOSE
WHICH CHILLED BARNEY VOGEL'S BLOOD AND GAVE HIM A CHRISTMAS GHOST STORY
Barney Vogel, cashier of the Monticello National Bank likes roast goose, but he has passed a resolution that hereafter he will buy his Christmas goose ready-dressed instead of "on the hoof."

Last week when the live goose he had engaged was brought in he undertook to carry it home. As usual at the holiday season, he had a number of packages to carry, and when he finally got the goose under his arm he was in poor condition to subdue the bird in case it should become fractious on the way, "which it did," as Little Benny would say. He had not proceeded far until the goose succeeded in freeing its wings, and the rest of the journey Barney accomplished mostly with his eyes shut, for a goose's wings thrashing a man's face seriously threatens his eyesight. Reaching home at last, smarting with excoriations and in no angelic mood, he put down his package and proceeded immediately to the cellar with the goose. After hanging it up by the feet he cut its throat and bled it. Then he cut off its vicious wings and was proceeding to dress the bird for the oven when he had to return to the bank, leaving the job to be finished later.

On entering the cellar again in the evening he met a sight that chilled his blood and raised the gooseflesh all over him. The goose was strutting about the cellar as belligerent as ever and apparently challenging him to cut his throat again if he dared. Half doubting his own senses, Barney came upstairs and called his son Bion.

"Bion," said he, "you know what I did to that goose. Go down the cellar and tell me what you see."

Bion started down but sat down on the first step, stupefied with amazement, for the goose was advancing to meet him with outstretched neck and threatening hiss—and its wings were spread and flapping!

Father and son retired for council, and upon investigation it developed that during Barney's absence up town a friend had brought in another goose for a Christmas gift and it had been turned loose in the cellar for safe keeping. It was the second goose that was making all the warlike demonstrations, and the first one was still a dead and peaceful goose, just as Barney had left it.

Heilman, Warrick County

Boonville (IN) Standard, March 18, 1898

A family living near here [Heilman] was alarmed by a terrible noise at the window, like something was tearing the window out. It so alarmed the wife that a physician had to be called. The husband, after [securing] up courage enough to investigate the matter, found it to be no more than a quail, being attracted to the window by the light.

Indianapolis, Marion County

Hammond (IN) Times, September 24, 1937

An Owl—Not a Ghost

It sounded like a ghost in the chimney at the home of Mrs. Martha Mayer here, but a neighbor investigated and released an owl from the flue.

Logansport, Cass County

Indianapolis (IN) News, February 12, 1912
Noisy Owl Makes People Believe House Is Haunted
A screech owl lodged behind the grate of an unused fireplace, proved to be the "ghost" which for eight nights disturbed the slumbers of J.E. Small, in this city [Logansport], and caused him to negotiate for the sale of his home. Mr. Small and his neighbors thought that the house was haunted.

The family was awakened nightly by strange cries followed by sounds that resembled groaning. When an investigation was made the groans ceased, but the next night they were heard again, and then continued for more than a week.

Finally the police were called in and one was detailed to stand guard in the house all night. He took up his station in the sitting room, while the others retired. The policeman was about to doze when he heard a scream that brought him to his feet. It came from the parlor and he rushed in to hear groans coming from behind the fireplace cover. Mr. Small came down and together they took away the cover.

A big bird, covered with soot, fluttered out, striking the officer in the face. It was weak from long confinement without food or water, and was easily captured. It proved to be a screech owl.

Shelbyville, Shelby County

Lafayette (IN) Daily Courier, January 30, 1913
Frightened by Owl
Scatters Kindling and Gives Farmer Vision of Haunted House
W.R. Webster, a farmer living south of here [Shelbyville] had an unusual experience while kindling a fire in his heating stove, and for a time had visions of a haunted house. He had placed the kindling nicely in the fire box when it began to scatter in every direction. The unusual disturbance was explained when a screech owl made its way out of the stove. It is supposed to have found its way into the stove from the flue.

Farm Animals

Chandler, Warrick County

Evansville (IN) Journal, October 26, 1899
A Ghost
Pat Bartley Captures It at Chandler
During the past few weeks men have been at work removing the bodies of the people buried in Woodward Grove at Chandler to an adjacent cemetery. With the removal of the bodies came many [weird] ghost stories and people who passed the grove at night time said that in the moonlight they could see white things moving around in the graves and among the trees.

Patrick Bartley of this city who is superintending a coal mine at Chandler concluded to investigate the matter. He organized a party and they repaired to the grove to await the appearance of the ghost. While enjoying a quiet smoke one of the gang looked up and exclaimed, "There he is, now!" Sure enough, directly in front of the men was something white and it moved around with considerable life. This caused some of the men to flee, but Pat soon mustered his forces and they made a brilliant dash for the object of their search. Imagine their surprise when they captured a real live white goat which had been making its home among the graves in the silent city of the dead. The goat is now on exhibition at a store and is being gazed upon by hundreds of people daily.

Petersburg, Pike County

Evansville (IN) Press, March 11, 1925
A goat kept at a mine near here [Petersburg] is found to be the "ghost" which was believed to have haunted a mine building.

Needmore, Brown County[20]

Indianapolis (IN) News, January 30, 1909
This Ghost a White Cow
While Michael Finley was returning to his home near Needmore last night, he saw a ghost. He was so badly frightened that he ran his horses for almost a mile, where he notified persons that he saw a large ghost near the fence in

a field beside the road. After Finley had gone home these persons went to get a look at the ghost, and found a white cow wandering among the trees.

Aurora, Dearborn County

Brown County Democrat (Nashville, IN), August 20, 1914
SHOOTS AT "GHOST," HITS SELF
Daily B. Driver, aged twenty-six, a farmer and stock raiser, was shot through the thigh of the right leg in an unusual accident. He is in a serious condition. Driver was returning to his home after spending an evening with friends at the Rising Sun centennial. While driving past a graveyard a white cow, that had been grazing near the entrance of the burying ground, started toward his horse. Driver instantly thought of graveyard ghosts and drew his revolver and commenced shooting, and during the excitement a .32-caliber ball passed through his leg, another tore a hole in his horse's ear and the third hit the cow in the neck. Driver is also suffering with nervous prostration.

Richmond, Wayne County

Seymour (IN) Daily Tribune, May 15, 1924
HUNTING FOR GHOST IN WAYNE COUNTY
Like White Cloud with Fiery Red Face—Along Lonely Road Near Richmond
Police here today were laying plans to capture Wayne county's ghost which has attracted thousands of persons each night for the last forty-eight hours to a [lonely] road north of the city [Richmond].

The ghost takes the form of a white cloud with a fiery red face. A still hunt by police was planned for tonight and officers have orders to "shoot to kill" if the phantom appears.

Richmond (IN) Item, May 15, 1924
HAUNTED ROAD GIVES UP GHOST
Spectre and Cow Are One and the Same, According to Amateur Sleuths
The Cart road "ghost" has been laid. At least, a satisfactory explanation of the affair has been discovered by several amateur investigators.

A group of young men from this city took the matter into their own hands about midnight Tuesday and established the identity of the spectre, they said yesterday.

Stalking along the east fork of Whitewater, shrouded in darkness they were startled by a white form moving ahead of them. Brave, in the face of the dread "spirit" they pushed ahead, and to their amazement and consternation, saw two white forms moving side by side!

Buoyed up by an insane curiosity which overshadowed any fear they might have had, they forged on and had little trouble in catching up with the twin "haunts" and then they had a good laugh and felt considerably better.

For the double ghost was a white cow with a black belt around her body giving the effect of two distinct white forms!

Somewhere in Indiana

New Era (Washington, D.C.), April 7, 1870
An Indiana farmer laid a grave-yard ghost the other night by shooting his old white horse.

Fort Wayne, Allen County

Fort Wayne (IN) News, February 24, 1902
GHOST STORY SPOILED
...Last night during the still hours of the gloom, after the patter of the raindrops had relieved the monotony of a policeman's lot during a storm, there was a hurry-up burglar alarm which summoned the officers to the Gerding & Aumann hardware store, at 115 Wallace street. Residents in the vicinity positively heard the burglars trying to raise the rear window of the store.

Officer Lavanway, armed to the teeth, with a dark lantern and his eagle eye at work in the darkness, sought out the aforesaid burglar at his burglarious work. The officer, careful in the meanderings, with stealthy tread made a detour of the premises. There were positively no evidences of burglars. While the officer was using his watchful optic his active ear was doing double duty. The ear heard something at work on the aforementioned window. There was a calm hush in the vicinity and the ear put on double duty. It was working overtime when another push was heard at the back window. In the excited stillness of the night Officer Lavanway had his imagination well oiled and his eye almost led him to believe that he could see someone climbing into the rear window to crack the safe.

The officer again pulled out his trusty gun and wandered to the rear of the store.

There was a dark shadow. The finger trembled on the gun trigger, but the officer thought he would work his eye harder and keep his ear alert before firing. He stepped to the rear of the store and his foot went kersplash into a mud puddle. This frightened the burglar and he ran away on all four feet. It was Waltemath & Son's delivery wagon mule, who was taking a walk around in the alley and incidentally scratching his seven-year itchy nose against the window pane. Officer Lavanway's slumber was troubled during the entire day. He was not having the night mare. It was a genuine attack of army mule.

Oakland City, Gibson County

Evansville (IN) Journal-News, November 22, 1910

GHOST DROVE A MAN TO VERGE OF DESPAIR

He Was Going Home at Midnight Hour When a Spectre Appeared in the Road

A local boarding house keeper, who also drives oil field workers to and from their work, had the time of his life a few nights ago, all because he is a little bit "skeary." Although his name is not William, ghosts are not just to his liking. Driving along the road, several miles from town—the hour was midnight—a white object appeared directly in front of his team. Another item was then added to the high cost of living, for human hair went up. Shaking in every bone, but with a little nerve left, he urged his horses forward, but that white object also moved faster as he did. Finally he turned around and headed the other way—but so did the ghost. With a prayer that the life insurance companies would care for his widow, he gave the thing a chase, and when he finally overtook it he found a very much winded old white mule. The mule was evidently lonely and all because it wanted company, almost scared a man to death, caused him to quit chewing tobacco and forced a promise from him never to swear or bet on a ball game again.

Rodents

Indianapolis, Marion County

Joseph K. Shepard, *Indianapolis (IN) Star*, September 28, 1932
THUMP! THUMP! THUMP! "GHOST" MAKES MIDNIGHT MISERABLE FOR CITY FAMILY
Five-Day Fright Ended, but Not Until After the Police Too Are Stumped by Knocks on Door
Thump! Thump! Thump!

There it was again—three distinct raps at the back door.

Five members of the family of R.B. Crooke, 1102 North Kealing avenue, looked at each other white-faced—the father, mother and three boys, two of them nearly grown.

Tap, tap, tap—gentler this time.

They had been waiting for these knocks. But none moved toward the door. Each knew without looking that there was no one there.

Since last Friday night as the city noises died down each night and the clock hands crept toward 12, the rapping, as if from skeleton knuckles, had resounded through the little house with more menace than the blast of Gabriel's trumpet—knock! knock! knock!...

But each time the door was opened only darkness graced the threshold.

The family, we are reassured, were not believers of ghosts but, nevertheless, "the sound was enough to send the goose flesh rippling and tingling." They assumed the knocks came from a prankster or prowler. After repeated incidents of the scheduled knocks, the family decided to bring in the police. They were desperate and even considered medical attention for the matriarch "who was approaching hysteria."

Patrolmen Wilson and Fischer arrived on the scene. They, too, threw the door open to nothing and decided to investigate: "No man nor machine would cast dishonor on the 'department.'"

The policemen began a search of the house that was a search in all the annals of recorded searches. And as they sought, the visitors with unseen hands, one after the other sought admittance.

In the garret and the main floor and finally in the basement the search ranged. The only living thing in the basement was a large gray rat which slunk off along a water pipe near the ceiling as the light beams struck it.

With a fine-toothed comb they went through that basement. The raps had ceased, the guests had all arrived. The policemen, sweating and dirty, were stumped....

[Fischer] leaned on the water pipe—and jumped. "Thump! thump! thump!" This time right near his head.

And the ghost was laid.

The water pipe sagged slightly and had a slight amount of spring. Near its end it crossed another slim pipe which turned and ran up through the wall in the casing of the back door where those raps had been sounding.

Near the other end of the pipe were plenty of traces of one Mr. Rat, who, by running back and forth along the pipe had caused it to strike the other, and the sounds thus were carried upward to the door itself.

Now Mr. Crooke and any of his family may open the back door at a knock and expect to find some one there. Mr. Rat is no more.

Richmond, Wayne County

Richmond (IN) Palladium Daily, October 16, 1920

A GHOST FOUND OUT

My grandma was awakened by a terrible noise. It sounded like someone was rolling down stairs, or else dragging something over the bare floor. My! what a dreadful noise! Well, up Grandma got with lamp in hand; she hunted and hunted till finally she got nervous; so she called my mama and they began to hunt together. Grandma lived (I almost forget to tell you) in an old fashioned house way out near Earlham cemetery on National road, with lots of cupboards and queer, spooky places in it. Well, Mamma looked all around with Grandma and was just about ready to tell Grandma that she must have been dreaming, when, not two feet from Mamma the racket began to rumble and rattle and bang. Then, it stopped almost as quick as it had begun and then commenced again. My mama jerked open an old cupboard, and there stood Mister Ghost, a big old rat, trying to roll an ear of corn down the hole into his nest.—Marlin Clair Bishop, 5th grade, Sevastopol school, age 10.

P.S.—I sent a story once before when Aunt Polly[21] was away and they printed my name Martin, and it is Marlin.

[Ed Note: Dear Marlin—Aunt Polly is away this time, too, but we've got your name right, this time, sure.—Editor pro tem.]

The main entrance of Earlham Cemetery is located on National Road in Richmond, Indiana. The cemetery was founded in 1861. *Author photo.*

Lawrenceburg, Dearborn County

Hammond (IN) Times, October 21, 1910
Ghost Is Rat That Sounds Piano Notes
Harry Steinreid solved the boarding house ghost mystery when he sat up all night Tuesday and found it was a rat that sounded the piano keys.

Evansville, Vanderburgh County

Indianapolis (IN) News, December 10, 1915
Rat Proved to Be "Ghost" that Caused Piano to Play
J.W. Blackman and family, living at 1315 Upper Second street, do not believe in ghosts. However, their faith in a reason for all things began to waver when their piano played every time they left the room and stopped playing when they returned. An employe of a piano house was sent for to investigate and see what was inside besides strings and wood. When the front was opened a large rat dashed forth. It was cornered and killed with an ice pick.

Sullivan, Sullivan County

Pittsburgh (PA) Press, April 9, 1916
"Ghost" is Raccoon
Andrew Singleton, a miner, has been hearing queer sounds under his house all winter, and although he says he does not believe in ghosts he began to fear the place was haunted. But the truth became known the other day when Singleton began an investigation. A raccoon darted from under the house and ran across the street. The raccoon had been gnawing at the floor under the house, where it had made itself comfortable.

Tolleston, Lake County[22]

Hammond (IN) Times, February 8, 1909
And now the ghost mystery is cleared. No haunted house in the old town after all. That is no house haunted by spirits of the invisible kind. But the house was a haunted one all right—haunted by "possums." One of our Tolleston braves shot one there and upon investigation found about a dozen

of them, more or less, under the house. "Now, what do ye think o' that?" "Wouldn't it jar one?" After all these nice gruesome stories were published in all sorts of papers and Tolleston received some undesirable free advertising, the whole cause of all this rumpus is an innocent "possum."

This story would furnish some excellent pictures for a moving picture show. Imagine the [climax]—a "possum."

Well, this ghost story was a failure. Let's try again?

Indiana Harbor, Lake County[23]

Hammond (IN) Times, June 20, 1937

Tiny "Ghost" Drives 6-Foot, 260-Pound Man from His Room

Policeman Joe [Filipiak] drowned a ghost in Indiana Harbor yesterday and six-foot, 250-pound Joe Wisniewski can sleep again and things are back to normal on Policeman Filipiak's beat. And this the story:

The policeman noticed Wisniewski loitering at 135th and Main street at 3:30 a.m. Sunday.

"Haven't you got a home?" Filipiak asked.

"Yes," was the reply.

"Did you forget your address?"

"No."

"Did you lose your key?"

"No."

"Then what's the matter you stand on the corner this time of night?" demanded the puzzled policeman.

"There's a ghost in my room. All the time I turn out the light and there comes a scratching on the pail. I can't sleep. I can't stay there!" Mr. Wisniewski shivered.

He finally consented, however, to take the policeman to his room in 3540 Guthrie street, where he unlocked the door to admit Filipiak but refused to enter himself.

"It's a ghost," Wisniewski warned. "My ancestors all the time scratch on the pail."

Filipiak's flashlight found the pail and in it a tiny mouse. The mouse blinked. So did Filipiak.

The cop's job was only [half] done. It was several minutes before Wisniewski could be persuaded to look into the pail. Finally he peeked at the mouse.

Clapping his hands to his head, he grinned sheepishly while Filipiak drowned the mouse and with it Wisniewski's worries.

BEES

Annapolis, Parke County

Tampa (FL) Tribune, October 6, 1907
"HAUNTED CHAMBERS"
The ghost of a haunted room in a residence in Annapolis, Ind., has been discovered. It was an immense hive of bees under the floor, who had made a solid comb, eight [feet] long and sixteen inches wide, containing 250 pounds of honey. This, however, is not so wonderful as are the "haunted chambers" to be found in dry counties.

Okay, this story actually took place in Annapolis, Maryland, but was misattributed to a small community in Indiana of the same name in a few Floridian newspapers. For a short time, Annapolis, Indiana, was creating quite the buzz in Tampa and other cities of the Sunshine State.

MONKEY

English, Crawford County

Fort Wayne (IN) Sentinel, August 22, 1893
KILLED THE GHOST!
It Created No End of Pranks and Aroused the Neighborhood
A Monkey Haunted the Farm of Henry Maguire and Was Killed by Threshers
There was a sudden termination of ghostly visitations on the farm of Henry Maguire, ten miles south of this city [English], on last Saturday night.

The ghost was supposed to be the spirit of a pack-peddler, murdered years ago by a family who afterward fled the country upon being convicted of barn-burning and housebreaking. Those who saw the ghost describe it of impish character, dressed in black, with a face of diabolical hue.

Many were the pranks it played. Fruits, vegetables, eggs, and other products of the dairy disappeared. Eggs were devoured by the ghost or were broken on the horses and cows. Horses were driven wildly about the farm after nightfall, screaming with terror and manifesting the most abject fright, and although shots were fired at the ghostly visitations time after time, the trespassings still continued. Several times the ghost was seen by daylight, but only by women and children and the descriptions which they gave added to the complications of the mystery.

Last Saturday there were threshers on the farm, and the ghost was discussed in every form. Several were skeptical, and they concluded to lie in wait in the barn, stationing watchers at various points, so as to make sure of a cross-fire should the visitor come. After two hours watching the ghost appeared. There was an order to halt and surrender, which was unheeded, and then two reports rang out and the ghost was a sure-enough corpse. Lanterns were brought and the prize was examined, it proved to be the body of a large sized monkey. Where the animal came from is unknown, as no one in the neighborhood ever owned one. The death of the monkey put an end to the ghostly visitations and the neighborhood is again at rest.

Chapter 2

TRICK OF THE MIND

A man who does not fool himself seldom cares much about fooling others. But the man who claims to have seen a ghost wants everybody else to believe in ghosts.
—Evening Republican *(Columbus, IN), January 9, 1931*

In 1874, the Second Ward School opened its doors to the children of Frankfort, Indiana. Located on Third and Wabash Streets, the three-story building of red brick and stone could fit 600 elementary and high school students, with an assembly hall for 450 and ten classrooms.[24] This new building addressed the demands of a growing population, a population that continued to grow and resulted in separating and moving the high schoolers to a new high school building on East Clinton Street in 1892.[25]

The building's roof garnered much attention due to its intricate towers and ornamental pinnacles made of iron. It is no surprise then that a ghost would choose to inhabit such a beautiful piece of architecture. In 1894, the *Decatur Democrat*[26] of Decatur, Indiana, reported that schoolchildren were fearful of the Second Ward School:

> *Residents claim that during the entire night a fifer's music can be distinctly heard emanating from the roof of the building, and some of the more superstitious claim that they have seen the form of a man walking near the edge of the roof.*

Some citizens attributed the paranormal activity to a man named Entrekin, a carpenter who allegedly fell from the school's roof and died. What could explain the fifer music? Entrekin had been a fifer in the war.

This stayed a common belief until 1902, when the mystery was solved by a tornado. As the *Indianapolis News*[27] reports on June 27:

> *The building is a three-story brick with columns, decking and similar old-fashioned fancy work on top. At night, when the wind cries plaintively among the nooks and crannies of the old building, the believers in ghosts declare that Entrekin's spirit comes out and stalks amid the columns on top of the building and sings to the trembling ones who go hurrying by on the sidewalks below.*
>
> *The tornado Wednesday caused considerable damage to the galvanized iron ornaments on top of the building, and the workmen, in repairing the damage, have discovered the ghost.*
>
> *One of the tall pillars was capped with an odd-shaped galvanized iron piece, and it was formed to produce a whistling sound, which, when the wind blew in a certain direction, gave forth a series of soul-chilling weird sounds.*

This postcard of the Second Ward School in Frankfort, Indiana, was sent to a woman named Ruth in 1908 after the ghost story was solved. The writer (possibly pictured) had no ghost to worry about. *Author's collection.*

The ghost mystery was finally solved, and the Second Ward School once again became solely an institution of knowledge rather than a haunted house—that is, until 1928, when the school was razed to make room for a new school.

Some hauntings can be explained away by tricks of the mind. Sometimes the most logical explanation is overshadowed by fears (especially at night), beliefs, history of the location, prior experiences, constitution of the witness and so forth. As the following news items show, there are many reasons—from the wind (as seen at Frankfort's Second Ward School) to the unexpected introduction of a new technology—why it simply was not a ghost.

Wind

Prairie Township, Tipton County

Tipton (IN) Daily Tribune, March 8, 1912
The Haunted House
Cabin of Pioneer Days Puts Forth Many Queer Noises
But the Mystery Was Solved When Structure Was Torn Down
On the Trenton McIntire farm, in Prairie township, for more than sixty years it afforded the subject for a great deal of comment. Up until a short time ago the structure was occupied, various families having resided there, but a short time ago it was decided to dismantle the building and this was done....

The farm is owned by Reuben McIntire, son of the original owner. For several years people who resided there complained of strange noises and peculiar vibrations. There was talk of "haunts," and some people really believed that maybe the old structure was tenanted by supernatural beings, and many were the weird stories that went the rounds. All the time the tenants agreed that strange things were going on there betimes. Ghosts and goblins appeared to meet for high carnival, and denizens of the nether world gathered in [gibbering] confabs, especially when the night was dark and when the wind howled and caromed through the tree tops. No one was able to explain the unreal racket and the stories of the strange doings gathered emphasis and detail by repetition.

But all this haze of the supernatural disappeared the other day when men assaulted the old log structure for the purpose of tearing it down. On removing some of the heavy sills they found a furnace built of brick. It was four feet wide and ten feet long. There were remnants of a charcoal fire in the place and a pewter spoon was found. There is at this time no one in that section who can recall the furnace and so far as that feature is concerned the whole matter is a mystery as deep as the forests of the early day.

John Prickett, a pioneer, occupied the cabin prior to the coming of the McIntires and it is believed that he built the furnace for the making of maple sugar.

Those strange noises and apparent incantations that have been going on there of recent years were due to that furnace and the caprice of the winds. A part of the structure had been weather boarded and the wind, finding its way between the logs and weather boarding, and into the furnace produced a noise, no doubt, that furnished a sufficient basis for the weird stories that found their way into the community.

Shelbyville, Shelby County

Indianapolis (IN) News, December 4, 1918
GHOST STORY EXPLAINED
Shelbyville Employers Say Wire Frightened Night Watchman
That the ghost at the plant of the Chambers Fireless Cooger Company, of this city [Shelbyville], started with the fear of a night watchman of darkness, and the combination of a wire and wind is the explanation of the affair that has been made by officials of the company.

From one of the ventilators in the factory building hangs a wire, by which the ventilator is manipulated. This wire hangs down near one of the time clocks which the watchman must punch on his rounds.

The officers of the Chambers company say that the wire was blown into motion by the wind and that as the watchman stood at the clock, the wire, making a rasping noise, was blown against his back. The watchman carries a lantern, and it is believed that he saw the reflection of the light from the lantern in the ventilator glass and tin, and believed that he was looking at the face of a spirit.

Logansport, Cass County

Logansport (IN) Journal, March 28, 1896
[GHOSTS] THAT WALK IN THE NIGHT
AN EAST END HAUNTED HOUSE AND HOW THE MYSTERY WAS SOLVED
GRUESOME SIGHTS AND SOUNDS
THAT MAKE THE BLOOD RUN COLD ARE FACED BY BOLD SPOOK HUNTERS
Weird startling tales have been floating about town regarding a haunted house in the Eastend. Blood-curdling cries, hair-raising groans, ghostly rustlings and stealthy footsteps, culminating in the fall of some heavy object on the floor with a crash sufficient to shake the building is a combination strong enough to unnerve the stoutest-hearted man and cause a timid woman to die of fright. All this and more has caused a house on Fifteenth street, the second south of the alley, on the East side of the street, between Broadway and Market street to be deserted by renters as fast as they could move out.

The last tenant to occupy the residence was J.L. Lytle, and he did not stay long. The ghostly visitors disturbed his and his family's rest to such an extent that sleep was impossible, and so he left. The house is old, and was not built on the lot where it now stands. It was moved from another part of the city and like most houses of that class it was racked in moving. It is a one story frame building with a long garret running the entire length under the gable. Part of the garret is floored and may have been used as a sleeping apartment. The stairway leading from the rooms below is in the corner of the room. On the ground floor are six rooms and the door opening on the stairway to the garret is in the front bed-room. It was in this bed-room that Mr. Lytle lay and saw ghostly figures pass, heard footsteps cross to the stairway, saw the door open, heard the rustle of garments and then the long-drawn sigh, followed by a shriek and the fall of a heavy body on the floor of the garret above. Then silence for a brief time, when the whole horrible scene would be repeated.

Last night two strong-nerved gentlemen [Dr. Cady and Line Pilling] decided they would solve the mystery of the haunted house. They started for the scene at 11 o'clock and arrived about an hour before the time when ghosts are supposed to walk. This ghost, however, was punctual. In fact, he she or it was about five minutes ahead of time. At 11:55 precisely the first manifestation of a ghostly presence was heard. A soft rustle broke the stillness, like the frou-frou of stiffly starched skirts worn by a woman. Then a long-drawn sigh, and the two brave men drew closer together. Almost immediately there was a shriek and a groan that froze the blood in their veins, and a heavy body fell to the floor in the garret above, shaking the house from foundation to roof.

Both men rushed up the stairway to the garret floor, but nothing was seen. They decided one should be stationed at the head of the stairway in the garret and the other at the foot of the stairs in the room below. The ghostly occurrence repeated, but their search was empty.

The climax was soon to come, however, and it surprised even the intrepid ghost hunters themselves. As the sighs and rustlings again begun to be heard the watcher below saw the door of the stairway open and the footsteps passed him. The door swung slowly shut and the shriek and the fall were repeated. "Come down: Line; I got him!" Dr. Cady yelled excitedly. As Pilling bounded down the narrow stairway six steps at a jump, he felt ghostly garments brush him, but his nerve [stayed] with him. "There he is," said Dr. Cady, pointing to the door, the ceiling and the wall in rapid succession. "See that wall paper, how it's torn and hangs down? Now watch the door," and he swung the door slowly as he spoke. The sighing sound was heard. The wind came rustling in just then and the door banged shut with a dull thud, shaking the whole house. At the same time the loose wall paper fluttered in the breeze, and like a tight fiddle string, gave a groan and a shriek. "There's your old ghost," the doctor cried. "How do you like him?" Pilling danced around and waved aloft a pair of old shoes. "I've got his shoes anyway," he said, "and I'll keep 'em for relics."

And so have all ghosts a being such as this, more the creatures of weak nerves and superstitious belief than actual fact.

Indianapolis, Marion County

Indianapolis (IN) News, March 8, 1890
THE GHOST DISCOVERED
Plumbers and Gas Inspectors Unable to Find the Demon in the Stove
Mr. and Mrs. George L. Paetz, 170 East St. Joe street, were almost ready for several weeks to believe that a ghost was hovering over their peaceful home. A month ago a queer noise was heard in their sitting-room. At first, it was supposed to be in the natural gas stove, but when they would listen it would escape them, and go into another part of the room. At times the ghost moaned like a person in great pain, and at other times it would roar like a great planing mill or a steamboat.

Plumber after plumber were sent for, natural gas inspectors were consulted, but no one was able to locate the strange noise. Mr. and Mrs. Paetz were about ready to give up the haunted house when John Keen, the picture frame dealer, undertook to find whence came the sound.

[Examining] the walls of the room in Mr. Paetz's house, Mr. Keen found near the stove a burnt spot in the wall paper. In the center of the spot was a cracked place, hardly perceptible to the eye. When a hand was held over the spot the noise ceased. The vibrations of the air through this crevice had caused the noise, and almost driven Mr. and Mrs. Paetz to believe in ghosts.

The hole was plastered up, and the family is again happy.

Hartford City, Blackford County

The Times (Hammond, IN), December 16, 1924

Hartford City's latest spook yarn has been exploded.

For several [mornings] in succession the office door [opened], although extreme precaution had been taken to lock it securely.

A man, disclaiming disbelief in the rendezvous of ghosts hired [himself] as a local watchman. Night drew on and a wind arose. Suddenly the door opened, cleanly unlocked. But, there was no one about. The watchman locked the door and sat down. Again it was opened. Repeated demonstrations and each time failure to find anyone about puzzled him.

Then he stood by the door. The wind whistled through the keyhole and the door opened. Close inspection proved the wind had literally picked the lock.

Logansport, Cass County

Logansport (IN) Reporter, September 27, 1897

A Haunted Parsonage

Rev. Thornton, of the A.M.E. Church Receives a Scare

Ghosts Said to Be Haunting the Parsonage

Strange Manifestations on the West Side

Rev. Thornton, the young and talented new pastor of the West Side A.M.E. church, is much perplexed at certain uncanny manifestations which have been made apparent at the parsonage for the past few nights. There is a peculiar something about the weird noises which are produced by agencies unknown and inexplicable to him during the stilly hours of the night in his residence, and until these noises are logically accounted for the suspicion is going to linger that there are ghosts in the house, that the parsonage is haunted. This bit of business is very disconcerting to the young preacher and all that he has been compelled to endure during the past week is naturally making him nervous. Last night these unaccountable manifestations of some invisible presence were so much more pronounced than usual that the young minister left the house precipitately, and he is demanding an explanation of the disturbance before he will be perfectly at ease in the matter. For some time noises have been heard in the parsonage at night. Some of the church members insist that there is no noise which a rat in the walls could not produce; but then, they don't have to listen to the disturbance as closely as their minister does. A few nights ago a couple of the young men of the congregation declared that they would stay in the house all night with the pastor to fortify him against any uncanny demonstration. That night there was not an unusual noise heard. The next night, however, and preceding nights the manifestations were repeated and redoubled in intensity. Last night, as stated, the noise grew simply unbearable to the already wrought up young pastor and he left the house. A careful investigation of the case is being made, and if there are ghosts over there they will be laid. If prankish boys are disturbing the minister's rest they will be laid, too, and if it is merely rats, there will be a general extermination of the rodents about the place. An armed guard will be set on the house tonight.

Logansport (IN) Journal, September 28, 1897
NO GHOSTS THERE
The Rev. Mr. Thornton Denies a Published Report
The publication of an alleged ghost story in an evening paper purporting to be a statement authorized by Rev. Thornton, that uncanny noises which disturbed the slumbers of the clergyman were nightly occurring at the A.M.E. church parsonage is regretted exceedingly by Rev. Thornton. He says that there is no foundation in fact for the story and that he was not compelled to flee to a neighbor's house for protection from the ghostly invaders as stated. One night last week he thought he heard a sound as of some one going down stairs. He got up and found that his ears had deceived him. He told the story to some one and it grew as it was repeated till it assumed proportions beyond all reason. Rev. Thornton came here two weeks ago to take charge of the A.M.E. church. He says that the publication of such a fabrication is likely to work upon the superstition of some and asked that the story be denied.

Logansport (IN) Reporter, June 20, 1899
Rev. Thornton Here
His Presence Revives the Parsonage Ghost Story
After an absence of two years Rev. Thornton, former pastor of the A.M.E. church returns to this city for a few days visit. Mr. Thornton is now located at Jackson, Mississippi, at the head of a colored educational institution. It will be remembered that interest in Mr. Thornton's departure from this city and previous resignation as pastor of the colored church was considerably augmented by the circulation of a ghost story which the reverend gentleman was wont to believe and relate to his brethren and sisters of the flock. Mr. Thornton, while not a believer in the nocturnal visitation of the supernatural, was forced to give attention to strange and weird moans that seemed to emanate from the walls of the parsonage just at midnight when all the world was deathly still. No apparition appeared yet the regular tapping and tread of the ethereal visitor were plainly heard and the young pastor fled from the house. These uncanny noises and moans continued nightly and the pastor became so worked up over the magical influences that he related the story to his congregation who failed to give it credence. Shortly after the young divine's departure to new scenes of labor the house was given a few repairs. When the cracks had been closed, effectually barring the wind from circulating between the walls, the ghost was no more.

Evansville, Vanderburgh County

Herbert Cecil, *Sunday Journal-News* (Evansville, IN), July 18, 1915
"Afraid of Ghosts? No, Rats? Where?" Say Six Maidens in Camp at an Old Abandoned Farm House
Are you afraid of ghosts?

Or do the shivers fail to chase themselves up and down your spines except when a tiny mouse appears?

Clanking chains and unearthly shrieks have no terror for six Evansville misses who are even now braving the realms of [phantomdom] in an old farm house six miles north of the city.

Yet each of them admits that the appearance of a mouse is liable to precipitate a panic rout or plain retreat.

Hazel Burrus, 18 years old, Dennison street, Howell, leads the merry party which has just finished the first of a three-week vacation at the old farm house. The farm house is the property of Miss Burrus's uncle, James Burrus, and has been unoccupied for three years.

Many tales have passed through the neighborhood about it. It is credited with harboring more than one ghost and neighbors tell of strange lights that flicker in the gable window after midnight each night. Three and a half years ago Jacob Hillman, farmer, committed suicide in the house by hanging himself after the death of his wife. Since that time no one has dared to sleep in the house....

The loft was the scene of the suicide and the place where the strange lights appear, yet the girls sleep in it....

They claim to have seen [no] strange lights, although they [lay] awake at night to see them. No strange noises have disturbed their slumbers and they believe the stopping of cracks has banished the ghosts of the wind from the house.

"We were not afraid the first night," Miss Burrus said Saturday. "But we were a bit uneasy, I'll admit. We stayed awake to watch for the ghosts. For myself I can say I didn't even feel a shiver—"

"Nor me," each of the girls chimed in. "Nor me," each of the girls chimed in.

"This place is full of rats and mice, though," Miss Burrus continued. "Ugh," sounded from each of the girls.

"We had to bring out some cats to keep them away," Miss Franklin said, pointing to three house cats that reposed peacefully on the floor. "They look sleepy, but the rats don't come around."...

"This old house was built when Evansville was only a little village, uncle says. It has stood for years. He was planning to tear it down and brought me out to show it. I thought it would be a good place for a camp, so I begged him for it. He laughed and told me I'd be afraid to stay here. I really believe he made the ghost stories worse than they were to tease me."

"Ghosts!—well there ain't no such things. We're not a bit afraid. But we don't want rats or mice to come around here."

The girls will remain at the old house for the next two weeks. They plan to make it their annual summer vacation home. Men are strictly forbidden and the reporter was hurried away.

UNCANNY SOUNDS OF THE NIGHT

Marion, Grant County

Muncie (IN) Morning Star, January 11, 1908
WEIRD SERENADE IN GRAVEYARD AT NIGHT
"Ghosts" Playing "Nearer, My God, to Thee" Turn Out to Be Young Man Taking Up a Dare
The strains of "Nearer, My God, to Thee," from a flute, proceeding from the I.O.O.F. cemetery[28] at midnight, a few nights ago, attracted people in the southeastern part of the city [Marion]. Those living in the neighborhood of the cemetery have been discussing the occurrence with a creepy sensation for a few days and children have refused to leave their homes after night.

The vegetation overgrowth and towering mausoleums make the I.O.O.F. Cemetery of Marion, Indiana, a perfect place for haunting. *Author's collection.*

The I.O.O.F. Cemetery in Marion is home to Civil War soldiers and Indiana leaders. One wonders if they enjoy flute solos? *Author photo.*

The sounds were heard on one night only and the affair had about come to be regarded as a mystery when two young men of this city, employed as musicians at a Gas City theater, came forward with an explanation. The strike of the street railway employes had interfered with the running of cars between Marion and Gas City at night and rather than wait until morning the musicians decided to walk home. When the I.O.O.F. cemetery, adjoining this city, was reached one musician dared the other to play a familiar hymn while seated on a gravestone. The dare was accepted, but the flute solo produced such a creepy sensation in the one who had to listen that he begged his companion to quit playing.

Indianapolis, Marion County

Indianapolis (IN) Star, January 12, 1914
"Spook" Proves to Be Man Drowning Under Bridge
"I tell yuh, boys, it's ghosts."

Patrolman John Mulvihill carefully scrutinized his running partners, Patrolmen Franks and Pfaffenberger, and unconsciously stroked his hair to see if it was standing on end.

From beneath the solid floor of the canal bridge on West street came a faint wail. It was in the early morning hours yesterday. The patrolmen, passing, were attracted.

"Help! Help! Help!" came from under the bridge.

Mulvihill looked around, then knelt on the bridge. His partners followed suit and they listened. The cry was more distinct, but very weak.

Frantically they wrenched the heavy double flooring of the bridge free, and dragged from beneath a half drowned man. He was all but dead from exposure.

At the City Hospital he gave the name of Val Moran, and said he lived on Washington street near West street. He told the police his name was Ralph Dugan. He is 55 years old. He said he leaned over the rail of the bridge to watch the water glisten in the early morning light. He became dizzy and tumbled in, and was drawn under the bridge. As the morning light sifted through a crack in the bridge he saw a girder and he grabbed it. He was almost dead from exposure and had given up hope of rescue when the patrolmen chanced to pass. He will recover.

Kokomo, Howard County

Muncie (IN) Morning Star and News, December 18, 1902
STORY OF HAUNTED HOUSE IN KOKOMO
Mr. and Mrs. Charles Abney, who have been married for three years, moved into a house a few days ago where a murder occurred about three years ago. Herman Schultz was killed in the house by Arthur Woolford, who is now in prison. Since the murder the house has had several tenants, but none lived there longer than a few days.

After they went to bed Monday night they heard weird noises, as if the place was haunted by the ghost of the murdered man. They went across the street to the home of Mrs. Abney's parents.

Next morning Abney solved the mystery of the haunted house. He found a gas generator just outside the house. The cap on the generator had blown off and the gas was escaping through the regulator. This made the ghostly sounds.

Michigan City, LaPorte County

Seymour (IN) Daily Tribune, March 12, 1926
GHOST NOISES EXPLAINED
Mysterious rappings and poundings that have bothered the tenants of the Warren building here between midnight and 3 o'clock in the morning were explained today as coming from a car plant next door where an immense sledge hammer pounds out iron bars. The foundation of the two buildings are the same length, Valois Bowes, owner of the Warren building said, and the sound of the huge hammer travels through the tile wall making the mysterious sounds.

Gary, Lake County

Indianapolis (IN) Recorder,[29] November 5, 1949
GARY HOT TAMALE MAN'S CRY—A "GHOST MYSTERY"
The mystery of the wailing ghost was solved here [Gary] last week. It turned out to be no more but Joe Allen, the leather-lunged tamale man.

Last month, the article explains, Charles Strong Sr. and his family heard the cries of someone asking for help. They tried to locate the cries, but their efforts were fruitless. The sounds disappeared on Sundays and during rain. The cops were called to investigate.

Sensing a kidnap plot, the detectives checked the warehouse, the property of a lumber company, two junkyards and several oil companies. But they could get no closer to the source of the mystery noise. It seemed to come from all sides of buildings at once.

DETECTIVES BAFFLED

Detective Stanton at length was ready to wager Mrs. Costley $5 that the sound was not made by a human being. On that note, the city police withdrew from the case.

But the ghostly wails continued. Finally Charles Strong Jr. and his brother-in-law, George Costly, set out in their car, vowing not to return until they had solved the case.

The two men proceeded from block to block, listening for the sound. They were at 15th and Broadway—more than 10 blocks away—when their search was rewarded.

There, seated on his motor scooter and selling his tamales, was Joe Allen, who lives at 2143 Washington. From time to time he would cry his wares in a voice to rival a foghorn. First he would yell "Hot Dogs" and then "Here Wee!" in a long, piercing wail....This last was the voice of the "ghost."

When informed of the "mystery," Allen acknowledged that he has a pretty loud voice, but said he did not realize it could be heard half-way across town.

P.S. The detective paid the bet.

Shelbyville, Shelby County

Boonville (IN) Standard, December 17, 1897

THE GHOST WAS CAUGHT

A suit was filed in the Circuit Court Tuesday that brought to light a tale of domestic infelicity not often met with. The Spurlin family and the Girard family are among the best known in the county. Among them are Harvey and Sarah Spurlin, husband and wife, and Mr. and Mrs. David Girard. They are each about forty-five years old. In 1893 the Girards were divorced on account of difficulties that arose between Mr. Spurlin and Mrs. Girard. A year later Mr. and Mrs. Spurlin lost a seventeen-year-old daughter by death. She was a beautiful girl, and well liked. Soon after her death the Spurlin home began to be annoyed by the presence of spirits. On [various] occasions there would be mysterious rappings on the windows, the doors and at various parts of the house, but always on the outside. When these visitations came Mr. Spurlin always made an investigation, and on returning to the house would tell his wife that he did not find anything, or that he did see something, but that it got away. These visits of the ghost of the departed daughter were the talk of the neighborhood. One night George Spurlin, a brother of Harvey, was present when the strange rappings began. Grabbing a shotgun and calling a dog, he dashed outside, with the result that the ghost was caught. Now Mrs. Spurlin sues Mrs. Girard for $2,000 for the alleged alienation of her husband's affections.

SHIRTS, SHEETS AND PAJAMAS

Muncie, Delaware County

Muncie (IN) Evening Press, July 23, 1914

MAN ESCAPED FROM HOSPITAL CAUSES REAL GHOST SCARE

A genuine ghost scare, one not due to overwrought nerves or too much blind tiger[30] stimulation, excited a number of late pedestrians in the southern part of the city a few nights ago, according to all reports. People in that part of the city were horrified to see a tall white wraith flitting along the sidewalks without making a sound. Everybody got out of the way, some jumping behind trees and others darting up the most convenient stairway. The cause of the apparition was not learned until later.

A big red haired man was taken to a local hospital for treatment. In the middle of the night he decided to get away. As he was unable to leave the room or to find his clothing he made a rope of the bed clothes, wrapped a sheet around his body and descended from a window in true moving picture style, making good his escape. And [he] hasn't been back since.

Wichita (Boonville), Warrick County

Boonville (IN) Enquirer, April 18, 1924

PAJAMA PARTY ALMOST CAUSES RIOT AMONG WOMEN

Two young men staging a pajama party almost caused a riot among the inhabitants of Wichita (as the south part of Boonville is known) on Wednesday at midnight.

The two—Herbert Hudson and Clayson Vote—found the night rather warm, and couldn't sleep. So slipping out of doors, clad in their pajamas they strolled about the deserted street with only the silvery beams of the moon for a witness—so they thought. But—

A neighbor woman looking through a window saw them. She screamed one word "Ghosts." Other neighbors heard her agonized cry, and they too saw the two apparitions stealthily stalking through the night. Windows hurriedly opened, and the doors began to bang.

The boys realizing the sensation they were creating rushed back to their bed, and they have decided that they will stage pajama parties in their room after this.

Huntington, Huntington County

Daily News-Democrat (Huntington, IN), October 11, 1897

SAW A GHOST

Fred Pohler Has an Uncanny Experience

It was nigh unto the dead vast and middle of the night. Everything in the vicinity of South Jefferson street and Etna avenue was solemn and spectral and still. The very air seemed laden with mystery, Mystery such as one feels when he lies abed and hears a rat scamper around among the rafters overhead. Oh, it was awfully mysterious. And the awfulness of the mysteriousness seemed to weigh particularly heavy on the mind of Fred Pohler, the corpulent clerk at Whitelock grocery. (N.B., Fred weighs 72 pounds.) As he walked along the streets named, he felt that shivery, shaky sort of sensation that makes the bravest heart quake, and has been known to move the strongest men to tears.

Was it a premonition?

Just as Fred reached the corner of the King confectionery, on South Jefferson and Etna avenue, he chanced to look over toward the S.H. Lipinsky residence, opposite. And right out there in front of the house on the front lawn in plain moonlight was a weird, gruesome object that would have made the heart of a modern coquette stand still.

Fred gasped, turned several shades of white and fled. Back toward the heart of the city, back toward civilization and the abodes of things substantial he chased; and he never stopped until reaching the restaurant of Purviance & Dial. He dashed into the lunch room, and in a high-keyed alto voice he announced to the astonished proprietor and a few late lunchers that he'd seen a ghost.

Expressions of sympathy were not wanting. Everyone was filled with compassion.

They all went back with Fred to the Lipinsky homestead and there found that the ghost was of the earth, earthy. It was a tall white urn, containing some choice plants, which had been covered with a sheet for protection from the frost.

And Fred said never a word.

Indianapolis, Marion County

Indianapolis (IN) Times, March 5, 1927

"Spook" Stories Got 34 Boys in Trouble

Weird stories of a "haunted house" where ghosts and goblins ruled lured boys into the home of Mrs. Hector Fuller, 421 S. Clyde St., according to testimony given by youths before Juvenile Court Judge Frank J. Lahr Friday.

Thirty-four boys, charged with malicious trespass in connection with $6,000 vandalism committed at the Fuller residence, were before the court. Only seven of them were heard and the case was continued until next Friday afternoon.

One 13-year-old youth said he went to the house to investigate stories of the activities of ghosts there. When he and others arrived at the house, a huge sheet on an article of furniture flapped. They thought it was "a ghost" and departed in great haste, smashing a window to make an exit.

Some of the youths are charged with staging a "battle royal" in the library, using books and expensive manuscripts for missiles.

Clear Creek, Monroe County

Indianapolis (IN) Times, January 24, 1928

"GHOST" DODGES BULLETS

The latest episode in the effort to lay "the ghost of the Red Hog quarry district," south of Clear Creek, was a shooting party led by Noble Sicoe and including six other men. Shots were fired, but the "ghost" is still at large.

Indianapolis (IN) Times, January 25, 1928

NIGHT SHIRT FLAPPING ON WIRE WAS "GHOST"

Some man who became a modern and discarded a nightshirt for pajamas—a man with a sense of humor, too—was responsible for "the ghost of the Red Hog quarry district" which has been laid by Sheriff W.S. Curry.

The "ghost" was a man's nightshirt hanging on a wire near a barn south of Clear Creek. Flapping in the wind, it gave a realistic demonstration of what the antics of a ghost should be.

In the last few weeks several persons went ghost hunting and many saw the bedtime apparition. One party of six men, led by Noble Sicoe, took several shots at the shirt, and reported the "ghost" retreated speedily and in good order.

Plymouth, Marshall County

Semi-Weekly Independent (Plymouth, IN), January 25, 1896

A GHOST STORY

Here is a local ghost and burglar story, which, while it constituted a very exciting night scene in the life drama of those who played leading parts, has not yet been made generally public.

A week ago Saturday night, a certain belated pedestrian, while passing the residence of W.E. Bailey, on the south side, saw what he verily believed to be a ghost. To an INDEPENDENT reporter he described the apparition as being very tall, and clad in a long white flowing robe which fluttered in the midnight breeze. He said the ghost was marching around Mr. Bailey's residence with stately measured tread, with its gaze steadily fixed upon a point in the sky directly over the house. The pedestrian stood spell-bound for a few seconds but recovered and hastily departed. He never stopped running until he got home. He was thoroughly convinced that no man could be out in his night shirt at midnight with the thermometer not many degrees above zero and live, and as he heard of no death in the immediate neighborhood he became absolutely certain that he had seen a materialized spirit from the world of the departed. There is another chapter to the story however by which the INDEPENDENT hopes to undeceive him and set his mind at rest.

A week ago Saturday night W.E. Bailey was rudely awakened by a disturbance on his metal roof. A large metal roofed dow window forms a sort of alcove in Mr. Bailey's bed room. Against the top of this window leaned a ladder, set there some time previous when the roof repairs were made. When Mr. Bailey heard an unusual noise on the roof at the head of the ladder his natural inference was that a burglar had just climbed the ladder and was crossing the roof to gain entrance to the house by a second story window. He listened a moment and was convinced. Step by step he heard the burglar move over the roof. He arose, grasped his revolver and went to the window. After waiting a moment the better plan seemed to go out on the porch where, he believed the burglar, being alarmed, would attempt to descend. But from the porch the steps retreated to the window. Hastily returning to the window Mr. B. thought he would wing the burglar as he came down the ladder, but the steps were heard to again approach the porch.

To make sure that he would not come down by the ladder, Mr. B. removed that means of escape and returned to the porch. Now all was still. Mr. B, now concluding that the burglar was entering the house by an upstairs window, returned to his bed room, seized a lamp, and with lamp in one hand and six shooter in the other boldly [climbed] the stairs; but when he reached the second floor all was still and nothing had been distributed. Completely nonplussed but determined to solve the mystery he returned to the ground floor and went out doors again to reconnoiter. Clad only in a white night robe and goose flesh he walked stealthily three times around the house without making any discovery. The burglar, however, could still be distinctly heard on the roof.

Mr. Bailey was finally compelled by the wintry zephyrs, to return to the house for a fresh supply of annual heat, most of his natural supply having been exhausted. He proposed to go out again and find that burglar but on Mrs. Bailey's advice he concluded to go to bed and let the burglar burgle. With the first gray light of dawn he was out to solve the mystery. This time he succeeded. He found on the roof, with teeth chattering, and shivering from head to foot—chilled to the very bone—a black cat.

Reflections and Shadows

Elwood, Madison County

Elwood (IN) Daily Record, September 15, 1905
Woman Reading Book
Reflected in Window Across Street, Supposed Ghost
Considerable excitement was created in the west part of the town last evening when a report was circulated through the neighborhood that a ghost could be plainly seen through the window of one of the vacant houses in that end of town. A large crowd gathered in front of the house in a short time, and looked with awe at the window through which a woman dressed in white could be plainly seen, sitting in a rocking chair and reading a large book. A man less timid than the rest remarked that ghosts were all imagination and offered to enter the house and find out the nature of the [illusion]. He and a companion entered the dwelling, but on looking into the room where the spirit was supposed to be, nothing was to be seen. Of course, the crowd was more awe stricken than ever when this [intelligence] was imparted to them, but just at this juncture the spirit arose and closing the book, vanished into space. The next moment a woman, the exact counterpart of the ghost appeared on the outskirts of the crowd and inquired of a gentleman standing there, the meaning of such an assembly.

The ghost was nothing more nor less than the reflection of the woman in the window of the house, and when this fact was made known to the crowd they melted away like snow when the sun strikes it.

Muncie, Delaware County

Muncie (IN) Evening Press, August 15, 1905
Supposed Ghost Explained Away
By Patrolman Beall After Making an Investigation Into the Case
The supposed "ghost," which has been causing wonderment among the superstitiously inclined residents of the neighborhood of Hoyt avenue and Ninth street, has been explained away by Patrolman Beall, who, after an investigation, has found that the "ghost" is really nothing more nor less than the play of the rays of an electric light through the branches of one of the trees surrounding the house.

Mitchell, Lawrence County

Greencastle (IN) Herald, January 28, 1928
Mitchell Graveyard "Ghost" Solved
The Mitchell grave yard "ghost" story has gone the way of all "ghost" stories. The mystery has been solved, and no longer will farmers [and] others blaze away with shotguns at the spectral light.

It developed that lights from passing automobiles rounding a curve near the graveyard, cast reflections which are in turn reflected from the white gravestones.

Many superstitious persons were treated to chills and thrills while the hoax lasted.

Greencastle, Putnam County

Daily Greencastle (IN) Banner and Times, July 16, 1895
A Mystery Solved
Spooks, Noises, an Electric Light and a Nervous Neighborhood
For several days there have been quiet rumors, some not so quiet, that the Burns house at corner of College Avenue and Olive street was haunted either by spooks or by prowlers that had no business there, the house having been vacant for some weeks. Rev. Weaver, who resides just east on Olive street, has noticed lights about the house and other neighbors have had their attention called to the lights and reported noises. Some had become actually alarmed for reason of the stories, and their attention having been called to the matter, saw the lights as they flashed from room to room.

The mystery grew rapidly and reached the ears of our police. They at once set on foot an investigation and quickly solved the riddle. Marshal Starr walked down to the house and after passing around it broke into a silent smile and came up town. Policeman Donnohue went over the field and also smiled as he came up town. It is the opinion of these officers that the strange lights are the reflection from an electric light that hangs [on] the corner near the house, which shines through the front doors in such a way that it reflects into the other rooms, causing the seeming flitting lights noticed by the neighbors. Since the explanation of the mystery as given by the officers, the inhabitants of that neighborhood sleep quietly and sweetly and the haunted house on the corner of College Avenue and Olive streets is now but a thing of memory.

Warren, Huntington County

Huntington (IN) Democrat, August 18, 1892
JEALOUS
The town of Warren has an individual in the person of the editor of the Warren Republican who has evidently become jealous of the liveliness of Hunttington as reported in THE DEMOCRAT. He says: "It does seem as though Huntington would like to own the earth. For the past two months she wanted another railroad and then a street car line. Can the place never get enough? Now there is a young man in her midst that sleeps and dreams, and the very next night the dreams come true. Added to all this, Huntington papers now come forward and tell of the mysterious actions of what seems to be a bona fide ghost. Every night as the hands of the clock reach the mystic hour of twelve, near Englewood, a woman in black walks leisurely around and the startled inhabitants vie with each other in telling hair-raising tales about the prowling phantom. LATER: The ghost has turned out to be a small tree."

Rugby, Bartholomew County

Muncie (IN) Morning Star, January 29, 1909
GHOST IN THE TOWER
INVESTIGATORS TREMBLE
Three Nervy Individuals Are Put to Flight—Robed Figure
The American Society for Psychical Research[31] may be called on to solve the mystery of the Rugby ghost. The ghost is there, and almost any one in the neighborhood will swear to it, but the identity of the ghost and what makes the spook come and go are the unsettled questions.

For the last few nights a bright light has been seen to come and go in the tower of the United Brethren church, about thirty rods north of Rugby, a small village on the Big Four railroad, in this county. Some people tried to explain that the moon cast a light on some tinwork on the tower, but this was exploded, because the light was seen when the moon was not shining. It was also suggested that some house nearby was making the light and that it shone on the tower, but no house light casts a reflection that high and no lights in the neighborhood are strong enough to throw a light any great distance.

Retreat of the Brave Three

A number of the men professed bravery, but the women in the community have become greatly frightened and refused to allow them to investigate. Finally last evening William Weinland and son drove from their farm to Rugby and as darkness had fallen they noticed the light in the tower. It would shine with great brilliancy for a while and then disappear. They reported what they had seen when they reached the village and calls were made for volunteers to climb up the tower and investigate. Mr. Weinland said he would go for one and Arry Gilleland and his brother, Newton Gilleland, also decided to go. The men were about ready to enter the church door when an object all robed in white seemed to float around the corner of the church and make directly for them. They are all men of average nerve, but they did not stand their ground. Instead they fled as fast as their feet would carry them and returned to Rugby out of breath and thoroughly frightened. They declare they saw a ghost, a real spook and no mistake, and they absolutely refuse to investigate any further.

The story of these three men being pursued by the ghost was immediately telephoned all over the neighborhood and to this city, and now the community is more wrought up than ever.

There is a legend in the neighborhood that a murder was committed in years past near where the church now stands, and those who believe in ghosts believe that the soul of the murdered man is back to haunt the community. Another legend is that a lost soul, that of a man who failed to get salvation in the church before his death, has come back and remains at the church seeking peace.

Columbus (IN) Republican, February 18, 1909

A prolific piece of news up at Rugby has just been knocked in the head as it were. The good people up there had a ghost.…The ghost took the form of a light in the old church tower, and residents of the neighborhood were much exercised over the spook. But now the mystery has been solved. It has been demonstrated beyond the peradventure of a doubt and the statement can be made without the fear of successful contradiction that the ghost is the reflection of the light from a window in the home of Joseph Wolf, which shines on a piece of tin in the United Brethren church belfry.

Hammond, Lake County

Lake County Times (Hammond, IN), August 1, 1906
Al Wagner Sees Ghost
Uncanny Vision in Lonely Road Frightens Auto Party
Mystery Is Cleared Up
Sight of the Spook and the Stopping of the Machine a Mere Coincidence
Al Wagner and his party of friends claim to have had the experience of seeing a ghost. Wagner and a party of friends arrived in Hammond last night, being on their way home from a cross-country tour in their automobile. In the machine were two men including Mr. Wagner, and three women.

It was on the road between Schererville and Highlands, a fine piece of macadam, but lonely in the night time, that the party underwent the ordeal of seeing, speaking and passing a ghost.

Mr. Wagner is a strong man, one whose appearance shows that he is afraid of nothing, but in telling of his experience and that of his friends he said: "I don't remember the time when I was afraid of anything; I may not have been afraid last night but the feeling that overtook me and my friends is indescribable. I tried hard not to show it and if the people with me failed to see it, it was because they were under the same spell.

"Turning the road at Schererville that goes north, we met not a soul. Only a rabbit crossed our track here and there. Along many spots the road is lined with big willow trees. We had just passed a farm that was made lonlier by the lack of a dog's bark, when Mr. Reynolds suddenly grasped my arm with such a vehemence that I almost lost control of the steering wheel, and said to me in a hoarse voice. 'Al, look!' Just then the women in the rear of the car gave a scream and I turned partly around to see the cause of alarm.

Then the Engine Stops

"Suddenly the machinery beneath gave away and without applying the brake we came to a standstill. It had all [happened] in a few seconds. Reynolds was still looking into the sky. Nobody seemed to notice that the machinery had given out. I told them that something was wrong with the machine and Reynolds again took hold of my arm and said, in a hoarse voice: 'That's what done it, Al.' Then I followed his eyes and at last saw the cause of the fear and the trouble with my machine. Upon my life, sir, we were only a few hundred feet from the ghost that seemed to have his throne in one of the large [willow] trees. His size to me seemed to be immense. All kinds of feelings overcame me. 'Did he stop my machine,' I inwardly asked myself. I should have laughed at myself for seeing a ghost, but I could not get away from it. My companions evidently saw the same thing. We were still in the machine and nobody moving. Had I wanted to move I could not. Reynolds had me by the arm and my wife put her hand on my shoulder and held me down.

Mr. Wagner worked on the machinery and asked that his passengers look away from the ghost.

"I asked them, 'Do you believe in ghosts?' 'Never did,' answered Reynolds, 'but I think that one is all right.' 'What do you think we should do,' asked my wife. I suggested that we turn [around] again, look at the ghost for a minute and then turn in the [opposite] direction.

OF COURSE ALL WERE BRAVE

"We turned around and this time he moved. His features were indistinct, still I thought I could see his mouth open. Just then a stronger wind came along and the throne moved and the ghost party disappeared. As his outline came slowly back again, as the tree went into position, I was sure that I had the solution of our fear.

"It was not ghost but simply the huge outline of a human body made by the branches of the tree as the moonlight shone into them and as they were viewed at a certain angle.

"A large white cloud in back of the tree added to the paleness of the ghost. Every time the wind blew the ghost moved. I made my explanation in a joking way and it was accepted. We climbed into our car again after a ten-minute delay which to me, however, seemed like several hours...."

Mr. Reynolds handed the reporter a black cigar, saying, 'smoke this on me, and don't believe Wagner; he's kidding, and for heavens sake, don't put the story in the paper, we would never hear the end of it when we reached our home in Iowa."

Noblesville, Hamilton County

Indianapolis (IN) Times, July 12, 1933
GHOST LIGHT
Cemetery Mystery Only Reflection from Street Lamp
Yellow light that glowed from a tombstone in a cemetery here, and brought a chill to the superstitious has been shorn of its terror.

Nightly people came to view the strange glowing. It was said to have been caused by numerous radium treatments given the cancer victim buried there.

Finally, a man more brave than the rest walked around the cemetery and found the glow to be a reflection on the polished stone of a street light, half a mile away.

Elwood, Madison County

Anderson (IN) Sunday Herald, October 20, 1935
CROSS AGLOW IN ELWOOD CEMETERY IS EXPLAINED
Rumors Blasted by Sexton—Records Disclose More than 7,000 Burials
Recent reports of a "mysteriously illuminated" monument in a cemetery at Noblesville and exposure of the same by The Anderson Herald was followed by rumors here of a mystifying glow on a cross in Elwood cemetery. The rumor seemed to become gossip on "ghosts" and started curious persons "to see the glowing cross."

EXPLAINED BY SEXTON
Charles Starr, sexton of Elwood cemetery more than twenty years, heard of the fantastic tales. With a smile he dismissed all of the inventions of "mystery" and explained why a glow on a cross has attracted some attention.

The only noticeable cross in Elwood cemetery is a large gray granite monument on the lot of Mrs. Ellen Kutche, in the southwest section of the cemetery.

Mr. Starr explained that a street lamp at South G and Ninth streets, about 300 feet from the monument and at an angle reflects the light on the stone atop a mound, towering over others. It is the only light that shines on the cross. Mrs. Kutche's husband, Angelo Kutche, who died in 1926, and their son, Constantine, whose death was in 1932, at the age of 18, are buried

Even in the daylight, Mrs. Ellen Kutche's cross is quite noticeable among the gravestones. Her son Constantine is buried to the left of his mother. *Author photo.*

on the lot. At the son's grave is a small marker, and beside it is a large bush which casts a shadow on the monument as it waves in the breeze.

So, the "mystery of the glowing cross" is solved....

Lights and Electricity

Logansport, Cass County

Logansport (IN) Reporter, November 8, 1899
No Ghost There
Principal Martin Caused the Light in the Central Building
The reported presence of a ghost in the central school building Sunday night has been explained in the most matter of fact way. Principal Martin allayed all fear among the pupils yesterday by stating that he was in building at the time in search of a book and the light on the third floor was the beams from his candle which lighted him on his walk through the silent temple of learning.

Indianapolis, Marion County

Indianapolis (IN) News, October 15, 1908
"Who Haunted Health Office?" Is Answered
Strange Mystery of the Shining Light Explained by Pathetic Story of Dr. J.N. Hurty
The Mystery of the Shining Light; or, Who Haunted the Office of the State Board of Health, was solved to-day when Dr. J.N. Hurty, secretary of that board, told of his interesting experience at Earl Park, Ind., last night.

At 4 o'clock this morning those who passed the north side of the State House saw a bright light in the office of the State Board of Health, in the private office of Dr. Hurty, where he compiles information in regard to dread diseases and gets up bulletins about the nefarious bacilli which take so many lives. The light shone until exactly fifteen minutes past 4 o'clock and then vanished as suddenly and mysteriously as it had appeared on the stroke of 4. So much for the mystery. Here is the solution:

Yesterday morning Dr. Hurty went to Earl Park to deliver a lecture and to inspect the schools and take steps to stop an epidemic of diphtheria, which is causing loss of life in that city. His lecture finished, Dr. Hurty late last night went to a lodging house in Earl Park. He was tired and the thought of a good soft bed and repose appealed to him. He was led upstairs by the man who had beds to sell.

"Here it is," said the bed man, pointing to an old-fashioned bedstead concealed in one corner of the room.

"That bed is dirty," said Dr. Hurty. "Look at the sheets; look at the pillows. I don't like that." The bed man smiled. His smile might have been in derision; it might have been in embarrassment. Anyhow he didn't say anything.

But Dr. Hurty was tired. He looked at the bed with visions of microbes flitting through his brain and then he thought he would chance it. Without undressing, he spread a handkerchief over the pillow and jumped in.

Dr. J.N. Hurty served as chemist for the Indianapolis City Board of Health from 1890 to 1893 and secretary from 1893 to 1896. In 1896, Hurty was appointed secretary of the Indiana State Board of Health. *Ruth Lilly Medical Library, Indianapolis, Indiana.*

Dr. Hurty could not sleep and, believing that he was entitled to a good night's sleep, decided to head home. At 12:15 a.m., he took a Big Four train to Indianapolis. He finally got some sleep, until…

About 3 o'clock the Pullman conductor rudely shouted "Indianapolis," and Dr. Hurty once more told Morpheus farewell.

Then Dr. Hurty went to his office at the State House, and it was shortly after this that the mysterious light was seen. He had to go to his office to get rid of some of the lecturing paraphernalia which he had with him. Leaving his office Dr. Hurty went home and proceeded to go to sleep in the third bed which he had occupied during the night. He said today that he felt very well in spite of the fact that he had obtained his rest on the instalment plan and had occupied three beds in one night.

Elwood, Madison County

South Bend (IN) Tribune, April 13, 1912

BAD WIRING CAUSE OF HAUNTED HOUSE STORY

Elwood Mystery Solved During Making of Repairs

Elwood's haunted house problem has been solved after five years, and the ghost proved to be electricity. A 10-room dwelling that was formerly owned by Frederick Hatman, and which was built for a boarding house in the boom days of the city, has been unoccupied for years owing to the strange and uncanny happenings at night.

Apparent hammering of the water and gas pipes aroused the sleepers at night. Gas jets would light themselves at intervals, one room in particular being flooded by light as soon as the door was opened. A rigid investigation failed to reveal the spooks, but the house could not keep a tenant long, owing to the freak things going on within.

The property passed into new hands the other day, and in repairing it the workmen found that poor electric wiring was the cause of all the trouble. The wires came in contact with the gas pipes, the gas tips acted as spark plugs, lighting the gas at intervals. The hammering sounds were caused by the electric current contracting the pipes.

After removing the old gas fixtures and rewiring and building the freak happenings and noises disappeared.

Cambridge City, Wayne County

Muncie (IN) Morning Star and News, August 22, 1901

GHOST SPOILED BY AN INVESTIGATION

Persons passing the Cambridge City cemetery after night have been frightened by glimmering lights and shadowy forms seen moving among the graves. On Sunday night a belated traveler saw the lights and galloped into town to arouse the citizens. He believed the cemetery was being robbed by ghouls. An investigation led to the discovery that the persons seen in the cemetery were employed to watch the grave of a young man who died recently of a mysterious disease. Before he died he made his relatives promise that they would not permit a postmortem to be made on his body.

Porter County

Vidette-Messenger of Porter County (Valparaiso, IN), February 13, 1939

MYSTERY OF GHOST LIGHT IS SOLVED BY JUMPING SHERIFF

The mystery of the disappearing light at the Church dairy, near the Porter county infirmary, Sunday night non-plussed members of the Church family and the Porter county sheriff's office.

Returning home around midnight several members of the Church family saw a light in the dairy. At first they thought their father was in the place, but found him when they went into the home.

Sheriff Freman Lane and Deputy Sheriff Frank Johnson responded to a call to the Church place. When they tried to open the door the light went out. Sheriff Lane commanded the intruder to come out. When there was no response the sheriff and his aid broke in.

An intensive search failed to [reveal] anyone. Then the sheriff tried an experiment. He jumped up and down and the light went on and off. An investigation revealed the bulb was loose in the socket. Any vibration caused the light to go on and off.

Anderson, Madison County

Anderson (IN) Daily Bulletin, January 26, 1897

GHOST AT THE ROD MILL

But It Was Only Cotton Waste and Electric Light

Last Friday evening while the men were at work in the rod mill they were somewhat startled and puzzled by the appearance of an apparition that had the appearance of a human form hovering over the big driving belts that run the machinery. What was more startling was that it appeared and disappeared every few minutes for a couple of hours. After Tom Irwin and Tom Brown had enjoyed the fun for some time they explained what caused it. In the engine room about ten feet in front of one of the electric lights hung a piece of cotton waste suspended from a piece of wire. It had caught in such a way that it caused a shadow the shape of a man. Every two or three minutes the wind blew the exhaust steam of the engine down from the ventilators on the roof onto the big driving belts and the electric light cast the shadow of the piece of waste right into the exhaust steam just above the belt, giving the shadow that very life like or rather a ghostlike appearance of a man.

There were several suggestions as to whose ghost it was, but as Will Lumley was on the day run, they couldn't ascertain for sure just who it was, but Owen McMahan said, "Be dad, it must be McFee's ghost, for he knows that the belt needs to be fixed next [Sunday]."

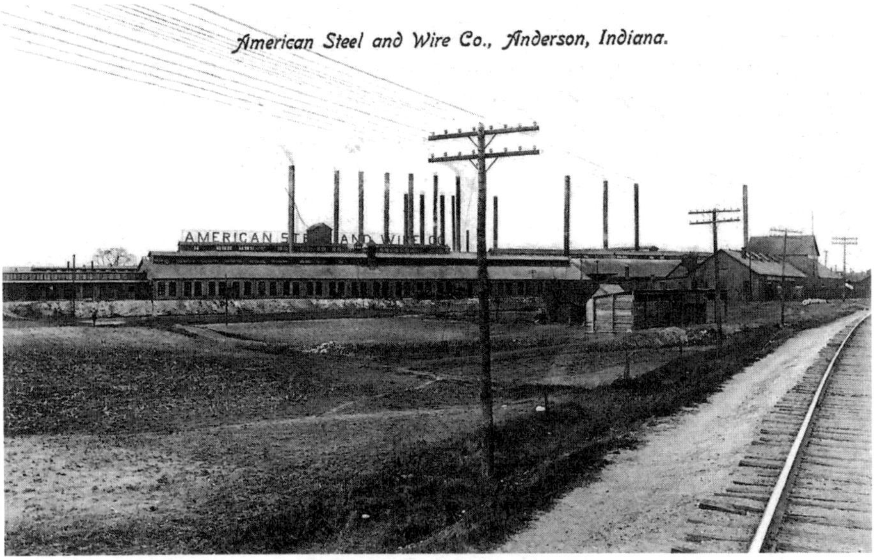

The American Steel and Wire Company of Anderson, Indiana, called the "Rod Mill" locally, produced nails, tacks, wire rods, wire rope and concrete reinforcement with wire hoops. *Author's collection.*

Evansville, Vanderburgh County

Evansville (IN) Courier, February 25, 1923

MISPLACED PORCH LIGHT CAUSED SCARE

Residents in Bray avenue enjoyed a real ghost scare last night.

Reports from the home of John R. Chase, 20 Bray avenue, at 8 o'clock last night indicated that something mighty unusual was happening in the attic of his home. Detectives Taylor and Patton were sent to the home, believing the call an ordinary burglar alarm.

Upon arrival the detectives found forty to fifty neighbors standing on the outside of the one-story structure looking at the small attic, from cracks in the weatherboarding of which appeared rays of ghostly white light. Chase said that he had lived in the home for four months and yet had to find an entrance to the attic.

A thorough search of the house did not reveal an entrance or a trap to the floor above. Meanwhile the neighbors grew more alarmed and the number of onlookers grew.

At last Taylor borrowed a stepladder and climbed to the front of the house. After tearing off a weatherboard, it was discovered that carpenters in repairing the porch Friday had torn off several strips of weatherboarding and had laid the porch light in the attic and tacked the board back.

By some accident the electric button was touched and the porch light, laying in the attic, lighted. Hence, the ghost scare!

Logansport, Cass County

Logansport (IN) Journal, March 13, 1898

GHOST TREED

Court House Mystery Solved by Gus Gerard

The mystery surrounding the court house…has been solved by Janitor Gus Gerard who [last] evening at the hour when the sounds begin, repaired to the loft armed with a lantern and a revolver. He had scarcely entered the room when the noise began and his teeth chattered violently. He had his nerve with him, however, and he began to investigate.

Along one side of the room two electric wires ran reaching the clock in the court house tower. These wires supplied the light for the dials at night and apparently the turning on of the light and its burning caused some vibration on the wires. Leaning against the wires was a piece of broken board, the end resting on the floor being very badly shattered. The vibration caused the board to vibrate in a way that produced a loud and peculiar sound. Mr. Gerard removed the board and is now anxiously waiting the arrival of the next court house ghost.

NEW TECHNOLOGY

Muncie, Delaware County

Muncie (IN) Daily Herald, July 30, 1897

FOUND THE GHOST

It Proved to Be a New Machine Operated by Compressed Air

The employes at the Indiana Bridge works have been laboring under a very peculiar circumstance for several days past and until yesterday it promised to lead to something out of the ordinary, when the cause was suddenly discovered. Some employe evidently of a superstitious nature, circulated a rumor to the effect that an unusual noise had been heard about the works a few days ago and that it was the exact date, day and hour, three years previous that a mechanic met a tragic death at the works. Naturally the following day, at the alleged time, those who had heard of the startling rumor, listened with interest as the time came, when it is said, the major portion of the workmen heard a repetition of the strange noise. The subject was afterward discussed extensively. President C.M. Kimbrough was interviewed this [morning] with reference to the interesting noise and he gave vent to a hearty laugh and stated that the unusual gutteral noise was occasioned by a new fangled machine used in reaming and is operated by compressed air and when in operation a peculiar sound is emitted. Mr. Kimbrough stated that the new device had been purchased recently and had been in operation but a few minutes each day. He also stated that no employe had met death in the works three years ago.

Seymour, Jackson County

Columbus (IN) Republican, January 6, 1910
OPERATOR THOUGHT HE HEARD A GHOST
New Telephone Line Between Columbus and Louisville Responsible for Fright at Seymour
George Hudson, operator at the Pennsylvania block station in Seymour, heard an unusual noise in the station a few nights ago, resembling the "honk, honk" of an automobile horn, accompanied by the sound of human voices. Hudson is not a believer in ghosts, but it took him several minutes to get up enough nerve to look about the room. However, he was unable to find anything and telegraphed the dispatcher that "something was doing in Seymour," explaining the strange noises he had heard.

This dispatcher let the operator worry a while and then told him over the wire that the company had recently installed what is termed "telephone-telegraph service" between Columbus and the trainmaster's office at Louisville, using the wire for telephoning that is used by the operators in speeding their code. The auto honk that came from under the table, the dispatcher explained, was the noise his telegraph receiver made when the telephone bell rang, and the uncanny voices issued from the same place. The operator had not been advised that the new service would intensify the voices to such a degree.

Indianapolis, Marion County

Calgary (CAN) Herald, September 20, 1954

"GHOST" IS LAID; HAUNTED TV TUBE WORKS NORMALLY

Mrs. John Mackey's television set is back home functioning normally after removal of the picture tube that had frightened her with an indelible image that looked like her dead grandfather.

The "ghost" appeared on other television sets of the Indianapolis area with the help of a station WISH camera. An electrician explained to the TV audience that the image must have been that of some television actor, burned into the phosphorescent lining of the tube by an electronic surge.

The "haunted" tube was sent to the manufacturers for examination and the station gave Mrs. Mackey a new tube.

AUTOMOBILES

Columbus, Bartholomew County

Journal and Courier (Lafayette, IN), September 17, 1947

GHOST TROUBLE

The Eerie feeling of being followed by someone he couldn't see so plagued Paul Dillon, of Hartville, that he halted his car in Columbus and hailed a police officer.

Sure enough, he was being followed and not by anything human. The car directly behind Dillon was empty.

The motorist decided that in pulling away from the curb he had hooked bumpers with the car parked behind him. He had towed the empty car for a block.

FLOUR

Brazil, Clay County

Richmond (IN) Palladium, April 12, 1938

DISCOVER "GHOSTS" IN AUTO WRECKAGE

Ambulance crewman thought they saw two "ghosts" in the wreckage of an automobile-truck collision near here [Brazil]. The "ghosts" turned out to be John Williams of Perth and George Williams of Knightsville. The crash had broken a large jar of mustard and tore a sack of flour which they had carried between them in the front seat of the car. The mixture covered them from head to toe. George Williams was brought to a hospital here in serious condition.

Fairfield, Franklin County

Brookville (IN) Democrat, March 16, 1899
Henry Kingery came to town [Fairfield] one evening recently for groceries. Starting home on foot, carrying a sack of flour, some lard, meat and coffee, he missed his bearings and took a tumble into Logan's cellar. Fortunately, he fell on the sack of flour, and was not badly hurt, but when he got out he resembled a miller or a ghost.

Dummies, Statues and the Like

Marion, Grant County

Evening Republican (Columbus, IN), September 7, 1903
Wasn't Afraid of Ghosts
For months since the death of Mrs. Martha Hamaker passersby thought they saw a ghost at the farmhouse, a mile north of Marion. No one would occupy the house, and even George Hamaker thought the spirit of his mother was haunting the place. William Price recently saw the "spook" late at night, but walking up to it, found it was merely a dummy figure dressed in woman's clothes.

Richmond, Wayne County

Richmond (IN) Daily Palladium, April 10, 1900
A Ghost
In the Wayne County Court House—A Would-Be Tax-Payer Gets Scared Out
A few evenings ago there was a gentleman desirous of paying his county taxes. It was long after night-fall, and there was a light blazing away in the

The Wayne County Courthouse, of the Richardsonian Romanesque style, was completed in 1893. *Author photo.*

treasurer's office. The gentleman drove with his wife to a point directly in front of the court house and got out, leaving his better two-thirds to hold the fiery steed while he deposited his atmosphere privileges for another year. He entered the dark corridor down stairs and started to climb up. The stairway obscured the light from the treasurer's office, and in looking about and above him the man saw the tall white figure that stands just east of the grand stairway. The man's hair began to lift his hat off his head. If there ever was a ghost, this was one, for it had human shape. He turned, with what strength he had left, and with rapidly weakening knees he fled with all the strength he could muster, through that doorway and out into the night, where his wife sat awaiting. When she asked him what on earth was the matter, he gasped that he had seen a ghost. He described it to his wife who explained that perhaps it was the Morton statue—and it was!

And now if that man's taxes do not go delinquent it will be because he gets a chance to pay them before dark.

Greenfield, Hancock County

Greenfield (IN) Daily Reporter, May 11, 1939
NOT GHOSTS IN STORE WINDOWS
Merely Two Tall Mannequins Wrapped in White Robes as Protection from Painting

Those passing the corner of State and Main streets have no doubt been attracted by the emptiness of the Goodman's Department Store display windows. In the corner window stood two tall figures wrapped in white robes resembling ghosts, but today turned out to be only display mannequins wrapped for protection from painting.

The Goodman store has completely redecorated their display windows from top to bottom. The plastic walls and the ceilings are now chalk white and the floor has been covered with Armstrong's inlaid marble of light grey, studded with seven-inch black stars.

Since being redecorated the windows have drawn quite a bit of comment from those who pass by. The Goodman's Department Store invites all of their customers to window shop their windows regularly. The windows are always changed once a week and the ready-to-wear window is changed whenever new merchandise is received, usually twice a week.

THOSE UP PAST THEIR BEDTIME

Fort Branch, Gibson County

Muncie (IN) Morning Star, January 13, 1909
HITS "GHOST" WITH A BRICK
Well-Known Business Man Is Now Laid Up with Bruise

The town of Ft. Branch, eight miles south of here [Princeton], has been agitated for some time over the appearance of a ghost which walked the streets at night and frightened some people almost out of their wits. Two or three nights ago this apparition came upon the wrong [man?] as ghosts have a habit of doing sometimes. This man threw a brick at the ghost, with such force and cleverness that the ghost was almost put out of commission. As it scampered away it emitted a groan that seemed entirely human. The usual quiet reigns now, and it is stated that a well-known business man of that place is laid up with injuries, which, his friends say, were due to a "fall on the sidewalk." He refuses to discuss ghost stories.

Columbus, Bartholomew County

Evening Republican (Columbus, IN), June 21, 1900
A SOMNAMBULIST
GHOST OR WILD MAN SCARES PEOPLE FROM PEACEFUL SLUMBER
Apparition, or Whatever He Was, Ran Like a Deer and Could Not Be Caught—Attired in Underclothes
A wild man scared the residents of the western portion of the city half to death last night between ten and eleven o'clock. He was attired in his under clothes and was running like a race horse. The neighborhood dogs began barking and following at his heels and they awakened the people from their slumbers. Several badly scared wives induced their husbands to go out and try to catch him but they were unsuccessful in getting within more than thirty feet of him. The man ran up one street and came back the same way, only on the sidewalk. One gentleman who resides on south Brown street, came close enough to the wild man to hear him breathing like a porpoise but failed to recognize him. It is this gentleman's opinion that the "runner" was a somnambulist. He was traced north on Jackson street and then he ran south again and disappeared entirely from view between Fifth and Fourth streets. No one was able to get close enough to discover whether he was a "wild man" ghost or somnambulist, but it is certain that if he makes his appearance again he will be shot.

[Later.]

It is just learned that the running wild man who scared the people half to death last night was James Culp, of the Democrat. Jimmy, so it is understood, was not asleep but was training to enter the speedy foot race here on the Fourth of July.

Sleepers and Sleepwalkers

Vincennes, Knox County

News and Sentinel (Fort Wayne, IN), October 19, 1922
Thought Wife's Ghost Followed Him in Auto
A young man living near Princeton who had gone a courting jammed on the brakes of his auto as he swerved around a thing which he thought to be the ghost of his deceased wife.

Behind him came the automobile of a companion and he waited. When the second car drew up, the youth was frightened again for there sat the ghost beside the driver.

The ghost proved to be a young neighbor girl who had walked more than two miles in her sleep. The noise of the first auto wakened her and she hailed the second.

The girl's father and brother carrying lanterns were found slowly tracing her steps in the road.

Shelbyville, Shelby County

Indianapolis (IN) News, June 30, 1916
Dreamer Fires Five Shots at Ghost Threatening Him
William McClure was asleep in his room in the business part of the city, and dreamed of ghosts. In his dream he saw a physician who had ended his own life coming toward him with the intention of choking him. In this sleep McClure pulled a revolver from beneath his pillow, and fired five shots. By that time he was fully awake, and the police soon were on the scene.

Plymouth, Marshall County

Culver (IN) Citizen, November 3, 1904
Jimmie Beldon See a Ghost
Jimmie Beldon, who runs Mrs. Hartman's night lunch-room, near the Pittsburg depot, had a bad ghost recently. At 2 o'clock in the morning he was awakened out of a comfortable snooze by someone entering the door. Looking up, still half asleep, he beheld the figure of a woman clad in white

from head to foot. Long masses of hair hung in tangles about her shoulders. Her feet were bare and her eyes fixed with a glassy stare on space. Jimmie knew that the unexpected had at last arrived, and for a moment was wholly deprived of the power of speech. The first thing he did was to make sure it was no dream. He then asked what was wanted. To this she made no more reply than if he were talking to a woman carved of snow. Seeing that a change of tactics was needed and realizing that the visitor was not there for the purpose of buying pie or coffee, Jimmie next resorted to a stern voice and ordered her out of the lunch-room. Turning slowly, she placed her hand on the door and vanished into the night as silently as she had come. The cold shivers were criss-crossing [Jimmie's] spinal column in terrible confusion, when he heard voices and a searching party came up and made inquiries concerning the whereabouts of a woman in her night robe. It turned out that the ghost was the daughter of a well-known minister of the gospel in this city. She has that trouble called sleep-walking, and this was one of her nocturnal excursions. When awakened she was of course greatly embarrassed.

THOSE BACK FROM THE DEAD

Logansport, Cass County

Daily Republican (Rushville, IN), August 19, 1910
THOUGHT HIM A GHOST
Reported to have died last winter in the south. Joseph Kilgore, formerly of this city [Logansport], stepped off a train here and surprised his friends. Several of them were so astounded at seeing him that they backed away, and it was some time before they could be convinced that he was a creature of flesh and blood.

Hartford City, Blackford County

Muncie (IN) Evening Press, July 8, 1925
LEGAL GHOST ON STREETS OF HARTFORD CITY
A legal ghost walked the streets of Hartford City today.

John Kitterman, who left his home in Hartford City to join the Klondike gold rush [in] Alaska, returned here for a visit with relatives.

No word had been received from him for nearly a quarter of a century and he had been legally declared dead and his share in an estate divided among the other heirs.

Indianapolis, Marion County

Indianapolis (IN) News, June 12, 1911

THOUGHT IT WAS GHOST OF A FORMER HUSBAND

MRS. JOHN FANCLER VISITED BY W. KINCADE AND POLICEMAN

SOBBED AT BIGAMY CHARGE

A ghost stepped out of the past and confronted Mrs. John Fancler, 306 North West street, this morning, when William Kincade, of Shelbyville, lifted his hat and said: "Good morning, Annie; know me?"

Mrs. Fancler said she did know the face and form, but she thought Kincade, whom she married when she was fifteen years old, died and was buried four or five years ago.

"I'd most forgotten all about him—I thought it was a ghost—I didn't know what to think," the woman told policemen, breathlessly. She sobbed hysterically and protested that a charge of bigamy, to which Kincade swore, should not be placed against her.

MARRIED ELEVEN YEARS AGO

Mrs. Kincade-Fancler was formerly Anna Burns. She is twenty-six years old and was married eleven years ago to Kincade. After the birth of the last of six children domestic life grew too strenuous for both. Mrs. Kincade left the home and Kincade became sick. He lay between life and death for weeks, according to his own statement, and when he recovered cared for three children who survived baby illness took much of his time.

He never had time to look for his missing wife until recently, when reports of her presence in Indianapolis as the wife of another man reached him. He found homes for his children and began the search, which ended with his greeting to his wife as she was engaged in her morning housework.

THOUGHT HE WAS DEAD

Mrs. Kincade, who admits her second marriage to Fancler, a machinist, says her mother informed her Kincade was dead. She knew of his illness and she says her mother had been in Shelbyville, after she left, repeatedly. The mother brought positive assurance of the death of Kincade, she asserts. For two years she has been living as Mrs. John Fancler, in North West street.

South Bend, St. Joseph County

Indianapolis (IN) Star, October 22, 1928
"DEAD" MAN RETURNS; WIFE FLEES "GHOST"
Several hours after Mrs. Jacob Kwitek, wife of a shoe cobbler, had been notified by police early this morning that her husband had been killed by a street car, the cobbler, a victim of mistaken identity, sought admission to his home.

"Who's there?" his wife queried in response to his knock.

"It's me," Jacob answered.

"Well, I'll let you in," Mrs. Kwitek replied as she gazed through the door window at what she believed to be an apparition.

She opened the front door and fled through the rear. Jacob sought an answer from policemen. They told him he was supposed to be dead.

The body which had been identified as Jacob's by the latter's brother, was that of Sam Begus, a gas worker.

Wabash, Wabash County

Rushville (IN) Republican, August 6, 1919
TWICE REPORTED DEAD
After having been officially reported dead twice by the war department, Michael Drake entered his home here yesterday afternoon, and his mother who did not know he was coming, thought him a ghost and fainted.

HUNTERS

Miller, Lake County

Hammond (IN) Times, July 8, 1910
MARSH GHOST TRAILED TO HIS LAIR
Down in Miller the good people who go to rest with the chickens have been making loud complaints lately about their nocturnal slumbers being

disturbed. Heretofore they always slept sound with the exception of when these three things happened: 1. Whenever the Aetna Powder[32] mills blow up; 2. On such occasions when a wolf from the Kankakee marshes[33] makes its way northward and howls all night; 3. When the reflections of the Gary steel plant light up their bedrooms.

Uncanny Lights Near Cemetery

Of late ghostly lights have been seen in the marsh in the rear of the old cemetery. Those of the Millerites whose business keeps them away from home until the clock hands near twelve and the gobblins are abroad have been seeing some mysterious lights in the nearby marshes. Coincident with the recent appearances of the ghostly illuminants it has been noted that the croaking of the frogs has almost ceased. Such unusual silence is a thing that even the oldest inhabitant of the town can't remember the like.

Swains who have been out buggy riding late at [night] and who have occasion to travel over the gravel pike to Hobart returned home early. They noticed the lights and when they danced up and down along the marshes timid maidens clutched their lover's arm and turned their heads as their teeth chattered and cold shivers passed through them i.e. their bodies.

Strange Doings in Marshes

Every one concluded that ghosts must be hovering over the marshes for not since the time the Pottowattomies left the neighborhood have the bull frogs been known to be so silent. This was the general theory until a few nights ago and mothers whose children did not behave were warned that the marsh bogy man would catch them.

However, the marsh ghost has been made a fictional character by Fred Schauff an engineer from Gary who is employed on the Elgin, Joliet and Eastern railway. The other night Mr. [Schauff] went down to Miller and found the whole town all excited as the "ghost" was said to be abroad.

Unusual Phenomenons Explained

Schauff ridiculed the ghost theory and about ten o'clock he made a quite little investigation for himself and after putting on his hip boots and tying a mosquito net about his head he went to the marshes and this is what he saw: Judge William Westergren in hunting attire hunting frogs. The judge was provided with a small gasoline torch. This he carried with him as the light blinds the frogs and makes them easy to catch.

Judge Westergren has been pursuing this occupation nightly for the past two weeks and he has caught hundreds of frogs which he has shipped to friends in Chicago. Of course his nocturnal expeditions were so regular that the frogs lay in wait for the jurist and they tried to dodge him by keeping [quiet] but the judge was too foxy for them.

As a result the Miller folk are resting easier and tomorrow a delegation will wait on the judge and ask him to leave off his nightly prowlings for a while in order that the town can make up for lost sleep.

Kratzville, Vanderburgh County

Indianapolis (IN) News, January 3, 1916
GO GHOST HUNTING
Men and Boys at Kratzville Arm Themselves and Search Wood
About fifty men and boys living in the vicinity of Kratzville, six miles west of here [Evansville], went in search of "ghosts" supposed to be in the woods near the village for the last week. Persons reported seeing shadowy figures and mysterious lights flitting through the woods at night, and the women and children had become so frightened that they refused to leave their homes at night. The crowd was armed with pistols, shotguns and clubs. They made a thorough search of the woods, but no ghost was found.

Evansville (IN) Press, January 3, 1916
GHOSTS WERE ONLY POSSUM HUNTERS
"Ghosts" which have terrorized Kratzville residents were disrobed Sunday night.

Lights which came and went in Elmendorf's woods had caused such a fright that women and children would not venture out at night—and even some men were skeered!

Fred Klenck, Chas. Kirkpatrick, Carl and Theodore Miller, Claud Franks and James Dugan Sunday night thought the time had come to drag the ghost out into the perpetual glare of auto headlights that illumines that section of the loop. They found that the "ghosts" were the flash lamps of hunters attempting to tree possums.

Those Intoxicated

Elwood, Madison County

Elwood (IN) Call Leader, October 22, 1912
Saw Ghosts
Passing near the Baptist church last evening, a number of women saw what they thought to be a dead man lying in the shadows and thinking murder had been done or suicide had been committed, and quickly called a man who happened to be passing. An investigation failed to show any signs of life and it had almost been decided that he was really dead, when he began to come to life. With the assistance of several men who had gathered, he was placed on his feet and started home. The corps proved to be a man perhaps thirty who had attempted to drink a saloon dry.

South Bend, St. Joseph County

South Bend (IN) Tribune, March 13, 1918
"Ghost" Is Arrested
Taxi Drivers Frightened Until Patrolman Catches Alex Bunis[34]
Taxi drivers going to the University of Notre Dame last Tuesday night were badly frightened by an alleged "ghost" in Cedar Grove cemetery. Most of the drivers were so frightened that they did not say anything about their trip along the Hill Street road. One of the drivers, however, saw a patrolman at Hill and LaSalle streets and rushed him to the cemetery.

The patrolman with his search light in one hand and a gun in the other crept along the iron fence on the cemetery and when the "ghost" came in sight jumped and caught him. He proved to be Alex Burns who was arraigned in the city court on a charge of intoxication. He did not know that he had entered the cemetery and said he was on his way home just north of Notre Dame. He was fined $1 and costs and instructed to stay away from the cemetery.

Lafayette, Tippecanoe County

Journal and Courier (Lafayette, IN), July 15, 1947
NO GHOSTS AFTER ALL
Reports by young people going to their homes late at night that they saw ghosts in the I.O.O.F. cemetery and were frightened, resulted in some of the more brave, making an investigation. It was not ghosts, according to a report made to the police. Instead it was learned that the ghosts were really two men and a woman sitting on a tombstone drinking beer. The informant said it was not just on one night but almost every night at the same hour. Police have been asked to investigate.

THOSE ARRESTING OR ARRESTED

Indianapolis, Marion County

Lafayette (IN) Journal and Courier, February 2, 1932
GHOST PROVES TO BE WHITE PAINT VICTIM
A ghost was roaming about the northern edge of Indianapolis, said a telephone call to headquarters last night.

Deputy sheriffs found John McCarthy, 24, Noblesville, covered from head to foot with white paint. An automobile in which he had been riding, loaded with paint, had overturned.

The officers took him to jail on a charge of drunkenness. The driver of the automobile escaped.

Lawrenceburg, Dearborn County

Muncie (IN) Evening Press, October 21, 1911
OFFICIALS ARREST "GHOST" AT ABANDONED TOLLGATE
The county officials arrested Thomas J. Dennerline, age sixty-four in the employ of Henry J. Ellenhausen, [ex-superintendent] of the county infirmary. Dennerline was found hiding in the old abandoned house of the tollgate keeper, on the Manchester pike, with a large corn knife, a jug of whiskey, an old Indian skull and a black, [loose] flowing cloak and hoodlike covering. For a week or more a hooded "ghost" robed in black, has been

frightening pedestrians near the old tollhouse. The "ghost" would suddenly appear at the side of men and women and, after accompanying them a short distance, or until the approach of another person, it would vanish. At 12 o'clock each night the neighbors have been aroused by screams and shrieks coming from the old tollhouse, but it is now believed that the mystery of the ghost has been solved.

Benton Township, Elkhart County

Indianapolis (IN) News, July 21, 1896
A Ghost Ten Feet in [Height]
Resembles an Old Man with White Whiskers
The farmers of Benton township are considerably wrought up over the antics of an alleged ghost which is supposed to haunt a deserted church and graveyard, located seven miles southwest of here [Goshen]. The parsonage, which is situated close to the church, and which is vacant, is also said to be haunted by the specter, which was first seen by John W. French and wife while they were returning home from a visit in the neighborhood. The ghost is said to be about eight feet high and to resemble an old man with long, white beard, dressed in white and carrying a club. While it appears in the form of a man, however, it is transparent, and makes a noise resembling thunder. It advances rapidly upon travelers until about ten feet from them, when it suddenly disappears.

The ghost frightened William M. Moon last Thursday night so that he has been under the care of a physician ever since. A searching party went out last night, armed with shotguns, looking for the specter, and it was seen several times at a distance, and each time was greeted with a volley from the shotguns of the pursuers, but each time it disappeared, only to immediately re-appear in a different locality. Another posse will go out tonight, which will be divided into groups of two and three persons, stationed one hundred yards apart.

Quite a number in the neighborhood refuse to go on these expeditions, fearing dire results. Some of the neighbors say that the spirit resembles an old man who was murdered some ten years ago in that locality, save in [height]. Quite likely, however, the affrighted spectators, overestimate in this particular.

Indianapolis (IN) News, July 23, 1896
THE GHOST WELL LASHED
THE SPECTER HAUNTING BENTON TOWNSHIP BAGGED
The ghost which has been troubling the farmers of Benton township, this county, has at last been caught. He proved to be a man resembling a tramp in appearance. Searching parties went out last night and the night before.

Men visited the site of the haunting and broke into groups of two to three. Among these men was Mr. William Hanman.

He [Hanman] sprang upon the suspicious object, which proved to be a man carrying a white sheet, and also a peculiar whistle which, when blown, emitted a sound resembling thunder. Mr. Hanman immediately called his companions, and a consultation was held over what should be done with the fellow, who maintained an obstinate silence, and refused to answer any questions. It was finally decided to administrator forty lashes, after which he was permitted to go his way.

What his object could have been is a mystery. There is a suspicion that he was employed by a shrewd farmer to play "ghost," so that the parsonage, which is located close to the church, might be purchased for a song. Another theory is, that the "ghost" was hired by an amateur detective to frighten a man who is under suspicion of having committed murder about ten years ago, hoping thereby to extort a confession form the accused.

Lapel, Madison County

Anderson (IN) Herald, August 5, 1905
SPOOK THOUGHT NOW A THING OF PAST
Lapel People Are Satisfied that It's No Ghost that Looks in Windows
Many Lapel people have firmly believed for the past month that the town was infested with spooks and the belief had reached such proportions that the small boy was afraid to go out after dark. Rumors had been afloat in the town for the past two months that mysterious figures could be seen at windows in various parts of the village. One glance at the mysterious face was all that could be gotten when it would fade away and be seen no more. At first the incredulous [laughed] at the idea of spooks out so persistent was the night visitor that many became firm believers.

The spook theory however was exploded when Harry Wilcox found a fellow peeping in at his window and by a quick movement got between the intruder and the street. The fellow however stumbled over Mr. Wilcox clearly demonstrating to that gentleman that it was no spook but a man and a very live one at that. While the identity of the fellow is yet a mystery, yet it has been conclusively shown that he was no spook.

Greencastle, Putnam County

Evansville (IN) Journal-News, March 4, 1903
GREENCASTLE GHOST PUTS MAN IN JAIL
COLLEGE TOWN'S SPOOK WAS A DETECTIVE
He Was on the Trail of Robbers of Monon Freight Cars
Claude Hampton, Night Car Inspector, Concealed Freight in His House
The "ghost" that has been casting its baleful shadow over North Greencastle for the last two weeks, has at last showed its hand with the result that Claude Hampton, night car inspector for the Monon railroad, was placed in jail, last evening, and others may follow him.

The "ghost" was a Big Four detective, who masqueraded in woman's clothes and skulked in a ghostly manner around the freight cars and the station in North Greencastle, alarming citizens of that part of town who had to be out at night.

For some time goods had been missed from cars that were on sidings of both the Big Four and the Monon railroads here, but it was difficult to get evidence against anyone. The impersonation of a ghost was a disagreeable task on the cold nights, but the detective stayed with it and finally won.

Hampton's house was searched, and in it was found a wagonload of valuable freight. There were sacks of coffee, dress suits, women's dress goods, groceries and all kinds of wearing apparel. The stuff was hauled to the mayor's office, where it will be sorted out and shipped to its owners if possible, after it has been used as evidence

Relatives of Hampton were watched and some goods were found in their house. They were subjected to a "sweating" process, last night, and developments in the way of further hiding places are expected. One of the men examined was one who was the worst scared by the ghost, running into it one dark night on the railroad.

Rushville, Rush County

Indianapolis (IN) News, January 5, 1931

Ghost in Cemetery Is Only Police Chief Lying in Wait

Avery Corn and Elvin Beach fled from a "gun-shooting ghost" in the East Hill cemetery here [Rushville]. The "ghost" proved to be the chief of police, who had been lying in wait to see who would claim a quantity of stolen alcohol hidden under a small bridge in the cemetery. When Corn and Beach appeared, police surprised and caught them after a chase.

Opposite: East Hill Cemetery of Rushville, Indiana, has two small bridges. Could this one have been the location of the mistaken ghost? *Author photo.*

Above: The historic East Hill Cemetery is home to many of Rush County's founders and famous covered bridge builders. *Author photo.*

Bloomington, Monroe County

Indiana Daily Times (Indianapolis, IN), February 21, 1921

BLOOMINGTON PEEPER PROVES TO BE WOMAN

The "ghost" which has kept this city in a furor by terrorizing citizens of the east and west ends of Bloomington the last two weeks has been captured by the police.

It had been seen peeping in at windows; many people had been frightened, and one man who held a night job resigned his position because of the apparition, while the children of the city were afraid to appear on the street.

The mystery was clarified when the police arrested a married woman who lives in Lincoln street on information received over the telephone that some one was peeping in windows on East Smith avenue.

Evansville, Vanderburgh County

Evansville (IN) Journal, February 15, 1898
For Ghosts
He Fired His Gun as He Went Through the Bridge
Walker Adams walked through the old covered Salt Wells bridge Sunday night. He said the lights were out and he being afraid of ghosts, pulled his gun and fired four shots, as he says, to "clear it out." He met Officer Wolf at the other end and was arrested for carrying concealed weapons.

Judge Winfrey fined him $1 and costs yesterday morning.

Chapter 3

PRANKSTERS

The next fellow who starts a ghost story is likely to get all that is coming to him.
—Elwood (IN) Call Leader, *January 30, 1907*

In 1917, Hope Hospital of Fort Wayne moved from Barr and Washington Streets to West Lewis Street, moving out of the previous Oliver Hanna homestead.[35] Soon after, reports of a "ghost" spread across the city. Many gathered to catch a glimpse of a "light flitting from room to room" at the old Hope Hospital. The *Fort Wayne Daily News*,[36] referring to the ghost as a joker, questioned the ghost's fashion choices but applauded its use of current technology in an article on September 5, 1917:

> *The Hope hospital ghost is behind the fashion in the matter of garments, for it wears the same old flowing robes and makes the same appealing gestures the ghosts have made for ages, but when it comes to lighting equipment this ghost is a new 1918 model. He carries an electric flashlight of a bright red color. He's tricky though, for he carries the light in front, knowing that Fort Wayneites are so accustomed to seeing red tail lights on automobiles they will think he is going instead of coming, and before they realize that he is on their trail he can grab them by their upstanding hair and whisper the usual ghostly words of warning.*

The *Fort Wayne Daily News* reported large crowds gathering, and rumor had it, they were expected to return with clubs and bricks. Chief Lenz of the police, when asked if there would be an investigation, told the newspaper that he would not remove men from other calls:

> *There may have been spirits in some of the crowd who saw the thing last night, but there was no ghost. The street lights sometimes cast strange shadows and especially so on old buildings. As far as I am concerned nothing will be done by the department toward catching the practical joker who has been fooling a lot of people. The greatest surprise to me is that several newspaper reporters fell for it. If there was a "ghost" there, an elm club would have made him beg for mercy. That always works on a practical joker of this kind.*

On September 6, 1917, a front-page headline of the *Fort Wayne Journal-Gazette* read "'Ghost of Old Hope Hospital' Captured, Photographed, Cautioned and Discharged." The spirited individual was Fred Langenbaugh, who donned a white sheet to scare his wife. The problem that night would not be the "ghost," but controlling the crowd, even after the ghost was captured. Luckly, a midnight rain chased away the looky-loos.

Unfortunately, that was just the beginning of this ghost story. In the days following the ghost's capture, local newspapers reported that Mr. Langenbaugh collaborated with local police and the *Journal-Gazette* newspaper to deceive the citizens of Fort Wayne, and the matter was under

A visitor to Hope Hospital sent a postcard back home sharing their visit. No mentions of ghosts though. *Author's collection.*

investigation by the Board of Safety. Mr. Langenbaugh, the ghost, in an interview with the *Fort Wayne Daily News*,[37] clarified what really happened (at least according to him):

> *The Journal-Gazette and the police had better straighten out that stuff about me being arrested or I'll tell more about the affair than I've told you now. I have been offered $10 a night by a moving picture house to tell the whole and I'll do it unless the other parties in this deal treat me square.*
>
> *Talk about arresting me. Why the whole thing is a joke. The police knew all about it when they let the people gather around the building…They cleared the people out of the hospital for me last night and let in "the favored few" the Journal-Gazette speaks about. "The favored few" were police and reporters who planned the thing to fool the people.*

Mr. Langenbaugh explained that he had worked with others to originally scare his wife. After that was successful, the *Journal-Gazette* reached out for a repeat performance with the support of the local police. On the eventful night, Mr. Langenbaugh snuck into the building through a back door, posed for a newsworthy picture and was whisked away to the police station. "At the station," Langenbaugh explained, "Chief Lenz asked me to stand in front of the window to show the people that I was there and get them to leave the old hospital. The only reason I did it then was to coax them away from the corner of Barr and Washington streets so I could go home and get some sleep."

The whole spooky fiasco was a public safety issue, as the *Fort Wayne Daily News* reported later in the article:

> *Ten policemen were taken from their beats and stationed about the building to keep order, while several others went inside and cleared away the volunteer searchers so the "ghost" could move about unmolested. From dark until after midnight Barr street was packed from Jefferson to Wayne and Washington, from Clinton to a point a half block east of the hospital. Had there been a fire or a hurry police run someone would undoubtedly have been killed.*
>
> *In his explanation of the affair today Langenbaugh shows clearly that the police knew about the affair in time to have prevented the gathering of the crowd but instead of doing what they should have done, they connived with the local morning paper to carry on the hoax.*

Ghosts are all that is left of the Lyric Theatre in Fort Wayne, as it was razed in the 1960s. *Author's collection.*

Spiritualists believed that the ghost was not laid to rest and requested entry into the hospital to receive the message the spirit hoped to deliver before departing the hospital forever. Chief Lenz warned that trespassers would be arrested. The paranormal event, while complicated, captured the hearts and minds of Fort Wayne citizens. Advertisements appeared in following weeks for the Lyric Theatre's reproduction of "the affair that fooled the people of Fort Wayne." Titled "The Ghost of Hope Hospital,"[38] the performance occurred every Monday and Tuesday night (with unspecified run dates). Citizens who missed the original production could "find out how it was done."

The story of "The Ghost of Hope Hospital" is just one example of how commonplace ghosts are in the prankster's repertoire. It is a rather easy prank to pull. It is best to plan it after nightfall because ghosts are nocturnal. One just needs a sheet or can simply hide in the shadows. Anyone can moan and hit things, so sound effects are rather cheap and accessible. Most of the work happens in the mind of the "victim," who has become accustomed to the characteristics of the paranormal. The prank is even easier to pull off when a location is already considered haunted or is associated with a macabre event. In some cases, the prankster was not the original ghost but rather a copycat ghost joining in on the fun. Who knows, some of these ghost stories may have started with actual ghosts.

The intentions behind ghost pranks vary, with entertainment being the most obvious reason, whether to add excitement to the workday or garner a few laughs from companions. Some phantom pranksters deceive to protect or obtain property. Others are tasked with a ghostly performance as part of an initiation into a community. The consequences of these pranks, including newspaper notoriety, may result in dire repercussions. The ghost stories in the final section are also cautionary tales, some with fatal results.

Pranksters Playing Ghosts

Bedford, Lawrence County

Bedford (IN) Mail, May 20, 1892
The report that a lady in the south part of town caught a neighbor in her house one night recently, masquerading as a ghost, and kept him covered with a loaded revolver until her husband arrived home and unmasked him, is pronounced by all parties concerned to be a "fake."

Alexandria, Madison County

Daily Times-Tribune (Alexandria, IN), July 20, 1935
Ghost Scare of Many Years Ago Cleared by Perpetrator
Thomas B. Miller Tells How He and Companions Kept Residents of Pioneer Alexandria in a State of Fear and Excitement More than Sixty Years Ago
Solution of a "true" ghost story which mystified citizens of Alexandria 62 years ago and caused physicians making calls late at night to detour three miles out of their way to elude the rendezvous of the spirits is contained in a paper prepared for the Miller family....

Mr. Thomas Miller prepared and delivered a paper providing an explanation for a haunting, which caused excitement throughout the state of Indiana, at his family reunion. A paranormal phenomenon allegedly occurred each night at twelve o'clock at the I.O.O.F. Cemetery in Alexandria. Hundreds of visitors visited the cemetery in hopes of witnessing three strange spirits glide over the gravestones. Mr. Miller's story, published in the Daily Times-Tribune, *was presented as follows.*

This is the true ghost story told and solved to the public for the first time. At the time my tale begins, the I.O.O.F. cemetery was just laid out on three acres off the corner of my father's farm. Directly west of it, some 30 rods, was an old cemetery on my grandfather's farm. At 12 o'clock one dark night a Dr. Irwin, returning from a late call, arrived home, his horses covered with sweat, and reported a strange sight he had seen at the cemetery—three white figures floating along from the old cemetery to the new, their wings flapping....

As they came and entered the new cemetery, three white figures crossed and met them and all merged into one and disappeared before his startled eyes. Shortly after Dr. Sullivan saw the same occurrence, and the town was greatly excited by the reports of the ghosts' rendezvous seen by many reputable citizens. Physicians making calls at night would drive three miles out of the way to keep from passing by the cemetery. Others would go home early to avoid passing by.

The excitement spread over the state and crowds would come from afar to see the rendezvous of the ghosts and were often rewarded by the same scene

A gravestone inscription in the I.O.O.F. cemetery in Alexandria—"not dead but sleepeth"—might be translated as a warning of roaming ghosts (but probably not). *Author photo.*

at just 12 o'clock at night, while timid ones kept off the road after dark, and the occurrence was published in papers all over the country.

All of a sudden they ceased to exist. One of the ghosts had hired out to work up north near Ft. Wayne. He had been gone only three weeks when Bob Phillips was brought back killed in an accident, and after that the rest of the ghosts did not have the heart to meet again. My special chum, Charley Lines, died shortly after....

When father sold the lot there was a house on it occupied by Uncle Wash [Buckhart], Aunt Bet, Miller Buckhart and his family. It was moved to another lot and the well was filled up to about six feet of the top and the dirt caved in till the hole was about eight feet across. Now three of the ghosts and sometimes more slept upstairs at my father's house. A window in the gable end had a ladder up to it. We would strip the sheets off the beds, steal down the ladder and go to our meeting place, part of us to each cemetery.

At the given signal, draped in sheets and flapping our arms like wings, we would arise and run together at the old well, throw our arms around each other and as one, would jump into the well. Needless to say no one ever stayed behind to see us come out, but the next morning we were all in bed asleep.

Bippus, Huntington County

Daily News-Democrat (Huntington, IN), September 13, 1899

SHOT THE GHOST

Bippus Apparition Discloses the Secret of Its Visits

Here is a story told in connection with a prominent professional man of this city, and the ghost at Bippus. The professional man, in company with another gentlemen, drove to Bippus, arriving there at 2 a.m. They had a shot gun, and entering the cemetery they lay down, waiting for the ghost to appear. They waited so long that they got chilly and started for home again. They had proceeded but a short distance, when on looking around they saw the ghost. They retraced their steps to the cemetery and the professional man grabbed the gun and shot at the ghost. The ghost, which was about six feet from the ground when the shot was fired, began to rise slowly, and when the ball of fire had attained about the height of a telephone pole, it began developing and turned into a figure of a woman. The professional man addressed the misty figure and asked her what she was doing back on earth. She replied that her husband had been untrue to his promise and that she was back to haunt him, after which statement she disappeared.

The professional man was seen by a reporter and acknowledged he was out there at the time and that they had a gun and did shoot, but asked as a favor that his name be not mentioned.

Tribune-Review (Butte, MT), February 24, 1900
Ghost in an Indiana Town
Little Community of Bippus Wrought Up Over an Apparition
The ghost which last summer perambulated the graveyard at Bippus, fourteen miles northwest of this city [Wabash], continues to disturb the peace of that village. At midnight each night the white figure of a woman rose from the center of the ground, wandered listlessly about the tombstones, and after an hour or two sank into the earth. News of the apparition's coming was heralded throughout the countryside, and the farmers came for miles to see the spectacle. Many were skeptical and a few ridiculed the story, not having obtained a glimpse of the unearthly visitor; but there were many reputable men who contend that the wraith actually presented itself, and that they were witnesses. On one occasion some daring young men took a shot at the specter, but failed to wing it. Gradually the excitement died down, but recently the sensation was suddenly revived.

This time a minister, the Rev. Voeghtling of the Evangelical church, vouches for having seen the ghost. Sunday night, while he and Joseph Sell were driving past the graveyard at a late hour, the female figure, garbed in white, floated up from the earth, near the fence, and gave the horse the men were driving a severe fright. The animal reared and plunged and almost became unmanageable. They hurried on as soon as they got the horse under control, and for twenty rods the strange shape, the Rev. Voeghtling says, moved along on a line parallel with the road, and the frightened men saw it disappear near the schoolhouse. The same night at a later hour George Snell also saw the apparition. S.L. Emley, one of the most respected residents of the neighborhood, says that only a few nights before he saw the specter, which frightened his horse. The word of any of the men named is unquestioned, but neither they nor any one else undertakes to offer an explanation.

It is it claimed by some of the superstitious people in the vicinity that the restless shade is that of a woman who suffered great wrongs at the hands of her husband, and promised to walk the earth after death unless he mended his ways, and that, having failed to reform, she is executing the threat. The neighborhood is wrought up, and scarcely a night passes but parties visit the cemetery to witness the apparition.

Elwood (IN) Daily Record, December 8, 1906
THE BIPPUS GHOST
That Excited Huntington County People Has Been Explained
At last the ghost that made its appearance near Bippus, Huntington county a few years ago, and which caused all kinds of excitement for miles around in that part of the country, has been laid.

The Bippus ghost was a bright light that appeared in a cemetery one mile south of Bippus. The word was sent broadcast over the country and people drove for miles to see the mysterious light. Nearly all were rewarded for the ghost was not a bit particular and it presented itself whenever it was invited.

Recently a young boy attending school in the community told of a peculiar farm hand that worked for his father. This man had a companion and when the ghost was setting people guessing, this young man and his companion were known to be out late nearly every night and that both

A gravestone reads, "We will always remember you," in Bippus Cemetery, located two miles south from the community's center. We will always remember the Bippus ghost. *Author photo.*

young men spent much of their daytime sleeping. Where this one young man staid the women of the house suddenly came upon a peculiar costume one day. A sack with ugly looking horns was made to fit over the head and the garb would reach to the feet of an ordinary man. Two masks were also found and other appurtenances which would go well to make a costume for a real live ghost.

PRANKSTERS AND PUNITIVE ACTION

Indianapolis, Marion County

Greensburg (IN) Daily News, July 25, 1955

ROCK-TOSSING "GHOST" FOUND BY DETECTIVES

The "phantom" of Forest Hills is scheduled to make a flesh-and-blood appearance today in municipal court.

Miss Marybelle Ernestine Eastwood, 26-year-old maid in a home of the Forest Hills area of Indianapolis, admitted to detectives Sunday that she was the rock-throwing "ghost" who had the Roman P. Frey family in a turmoil for seven months.

Miss Eastwood is employed at the house next door to the Freys, who called police last January to determine the source of rocks being thrown against their windows.

Detectives tried on several occasions to locate the rock-thrower, and even though a rock nearly hit one detective, he was unable to tell from whence it came.

Best clue the detectives had was that the rock barrage usually occurred whenever one of the Frey daughters was returning from a date.

The mystery apparently was solved Sunday when Miss Eastwood's employer happened to enter the maid's room and saw a sling shot there.

She called police. Miss Eastwood told them she used the sling shot to catapult rocks from the basement window of the house next door to the Freys. Bushes outside the house were so heavy they concealed the window.

Miss Eastwood offered to pay for the broken windows, which Frey estimated at nine. However, she was charged with malicious destruction of property and is slated to appear today in municipal court.

Miss Eastwood said she was peeved at the Frey girls.

The next and final ghost story of this section, some might argue, could be placed in a prior chapter, but the sensationalized version involving an unreliable murder suspect is more intriguing than squealing pigs or cats. Context is needed before telling this ghost story, as it was part of ongoing, salacious reporting concerning the murder of Ruby Mauzy.

In September 1924, Ruby Mauzy was stabbed and passed before speaking the murderer's name. Her estranged husband, Emmett Mauzy, and suitor Aubrey Quinn had alibis, leaving another suitor named Tom Evans (referred to as "Black Tom" Evans in the papers). Evans confessed to the crime but later claimed he had falsely done so after being beaten by the police. Evans was given a life sentence but, with the help of reporter John Ellert and evidence pointing to Aubrey Quinn, was released in 1940. He died shortly after from a rare blood disease.

One minor character in this true crime story is Henry Chapman, a man who frequented the crime scene and confessed to the murder. The confession was dismissed by police as they believed Chapman to be too "feeble-minded."[39] *Along with confessing to the murder, he also confessed to playing ghost at the location of Mauzy's murder. Although some might argue it was just the noise of barnyard animals.*

Evansville, Vanderburgh County

Evansville (IN) Press, January 16, 1925

"Ghost" Flees Murder Scene, Pigs Squeal, as Cops Arrives

Ghost hunters? Evansville's got scores of 'em. They were out in force Thursday night to lay the supposed "ha'nt" of Ruby Mauzy....

The hunters kept a respectful distance from the thicket in which the fatal stabbing occurred, until the arrival of Police Sergeant William Barratt and two Press reporters on the scene at 7:30 o'clock, when the crowd that had assembled at the corner of Lodge and Taylor-avs mustered courage and trailed along to the lonely clump of trees.

Scudding clouds that hid the moon, a wind that moaned and rattled thru the straggly oak saplings provided a setting that any respectable ghost from Banquo's down to the best one that ever emanated from a modern medium's cabinet, might well have envied. Flickering beams from distant street lamps served only to intensify the murky gloom of the place.

Whatever the possibilities of the spot for ghost walking, however, they were not utilized Thursday night. There may have been too much company present. Possibly the "ha'nt," which has manifested itself only by groans and moans, turned up its eerie toes at the thought of trying to make itself heard above the snorting exhausts of the stream of cars that brought fresh ghost stalkers to the spot.

The sergeant surveyed the scene with no luck until he heard "muffled grunts" behind a fence.

…he suddenly shot his searchlight at the spot expecting to find a flesh and blood [source] of the noises.

He did find two hogs in a pen. It is Barratt's opinion that the porkers are the real culprits in the case.

Some of those living near the spot believe, however, that the "ghost" of the murdered girl has taken its last walk with the incarceration of Henry Chapman.…

Evansville (IN) Courier, January 16, 1925

LODGE AVENUE GHOST IS LAID, PEOPLE SLEEP

Sir Arthur Conan Doyle, Sir Oliver Lodge and Camille Flammarion notwithstanding the Lodge avenue ghost has been laid and Evansville is rid of its only up-to-date ghost.

Henry Chapman, 28, 2911 East Indiana street, demented lad who stands ready to assume any responsibility, whether it be that for murder or merely perjury, told police last night that he was the Lodge avenue ghost.

The man, with a wide grin, told how he frequented the fields about the scene of the Ruby Mauzy murder and how he thought that Ruby Mauzy had appeared before him and told him that he must do penance for her murder by impersonating a ghost at the scene of the murder.

"How was Ruby dressed," he was asked.

"In a long white nightgown," Chapman answered.

"What did she say?"

"She asked me why I killed her and I said because I loved her and did not want her to go with Tom Evans."

"Did you ever see Tom Evans?"

"No," he replied, "but I didn't like him anyway."

Assistant Chief of Police Norman Broshears last night said that Chapman was taken in custody yesterday afternoon on complaint of the people living in the Lodge Avenue neighborhood who said that he terrorized them by threats and his talk of the murder.

Pranksters at Work

Fortville, Hancock County

Fortville (IN) Tribune, August 25, 1949

Mystery of Old Haunted Brick Shop in Fortville Finally Comes to Light; Four Local Girls Scared by Raps

An empty building that stood on the corner of Staats and Merrill streets, known as the old brick shop, had the reputation of being haunted.

One evening about the year 1890, Gracie Bills, Nellie VanZant, Mattie Crouch and Mattie Arnett, known as the Big 4, who were always looking for anything to make fun. Strolling by the old brick shop, Mattie Arnett opened a door and yelled if there's a ghost in here rap 3 times. The ghost rapped 3 times, and as to what the Big 4 did, well, we'll leave that to your imagination.

The mystery of the 3 raps was solved several days later by Jules White. He and his brother, Frank were just moving in to start a wagon shop. Jules was in one of the rooms making some repairs, when the request came for the ghost to rap 3 times. He picked up a hammer lying by his side and hit the floor 3 times.[40]

Michigan City, LaPorte County

The Times (Hammond, IN), February 1, 1930

Solve Story of Ghost

Practical Joke Played on Workman by One of Other Employees

Identity of the headless ghost that struck terror into a workman at one of the largest manufacturing plants of the city [Michigan City], apparently has been established.

Many explanations have been offered for the [apparition], which John Laudwisch, the frightened workman, said chased him from the factory.

An explanation for the occult appearance of the sprite was soon forthcoming and related that steam from a leaky valve had been drifted by into a shape, which took on the form of a human body.

Now, it seems that the ghost was the product of a jokester. The workman was said to be sleeping near a salamander used to heat the plant at night; and was noticed by another worker who was aloft a crane. Taking some grease, the crane tender, dropped it into the salamander, causing a hissing noise, and awaking the sleeper, who arose in time to see the steam emitted.

Although [scared], the sleeper laid down again, and the crane tender repeated the experiment. Not being able to arouse the sleeping workman with his previous attempts, the worker scooped up an unusually large amount of the grease and tossed it below. This time, the grease crackled loudly as it hit the fire, throwing up a cloud, which the half-awakened sleeper, probably mistook for the ghost. The tapping, which he reported to have heard, came from the explosion produced by the falling grease.

Carbondale, Warren County

Jasper County Democrat (Rensselaer, IN), March 25, 1905
MINERS HEAR A SPOOK
They Come Near Striking Until It Is Discovered to Be a Practical Joke
A strike at the Triber coal mine, near Carbondale, has been narrowly averted. The shaft of the mine is at the foot of a hill, on the top of which is a cemetery. The mine has been worked back under the hill. While the miners were at work; and were talking of the city of the dead above them, a voice in sepulchral tones was heard saying: "For forty years I have lain unmolested. Why do you now disturb my long rest?"

The voice startled the miners, which as they listened, was again heard repeating the complaint. The miners lost no time in reaching the surface of the ground, where they told their story and refused to return to work. An investigation was made as to the cause of trouble, and a pipe was found, which extended down to the level of the coal, through which the digging of the miners could be heard. Some person, desirous of playing a prank, placed his mouth to the pipe and called down, as quoted, much to the fright of the men below.

PRANKSTERS PROTECTING OR STEALING PROPERTY OR MONEY

Terre Haute, Vigo County

Indianapolis (IN) Star, January 18, 1923
A CHASE AND A GHOST
Two miles from Terre Haute on a lonely road stood an old, deserted mansion, which folks said was haunted. One night last summer found me

taking a short cut through the fields, arousing a farmer's dog that would have torn me to pieces had I not beaten him off with a club, at the same time tearing my way through briers and brambles, and climbing a fence into a cemetery. The whispering pines casting their long, wavering shadows among the tombstones did not ease my wildly beating heart. I fancied I saw the dead walking about.

I was relieved on crawling through another fence into a field where cows complacently chewed their cuds. I shied around them and was making time when suddenly I felt something was following me. Glancing over my shoulder, I knew it! I started to run. My feet caught in the clover and I fell. Before regaining my feet I heard the bull's snorting and could almost feel its hot breath on my back. I must have broken the world's running record before I hit a barbed fence and fell over it into a deep ditch within sight of the haunted house.

When I could get my breath and was sure the beast was gone, I peeped over the top of the ditch. Horrors! Straight toward me came the ghost with its flowing white garments and black, socketless eyes. I was ready to faint when I heard the report of a gun and loud shouting. A [strange] sight met my gaze.

Men were surrounding the house. The ghost looking dejected, and very much human, was handcuffed by two officers. I learned then that it was a man playing ghost to keep people away from the place where he was operating a still.

H.G.[41]

Evansville, Vanderburgh County

Evansville (IN) Courier, May 4, 1899
Voice from Heaven Said Open Stone…
Trinity General Baptist Church a Storm Center for Seven Years, to Be Sold
Donor Churched Twice and Plays Ghost to Frighten the Congregation Away

Trinity G.B. Church
This Lot Was Donated By
Sister Mary A. Jones
June 10, 1892.

A white marble tablet with this inscription strikes the eye of one who wanders in the vicinity of Devon street and Uhlhorn avenue. It is inserted in the foundation of a little frame church with broken windows and unfinished belfry, devoid of paint, save here and there a daub of faded yellow ochre put on as a first coat when the building was erected. It has never had the second coat.

Speak to the neighbors and they will tell queer tales of the foundation of the church, of its seven years of ups and downs, of the end which is in sight when it will be sold on foreclosure proceedings in July. They will tell of a ghost which was seen wandering around it last fall, of the preacher who fell into a trance and ordered the corner-stone opened and the name of one of the original trustees and preachers removed because he had turned spiritualist and the church would not prosper as long as his name was left with the others.

But find the white-headed, sightless donor of the lot, now in her eightieth year, listen to her story and wonder at the persecutions she has undergone. But listen to both sides and you cannot reconcile their stories, but it will be a weird tale if you believe both or neither.

As the story goes, Mary Jones had not always been a Christian woman, nor had her ways been of the straightest. But she acquired money and was married. In fact she was married seven times to six men. One man by the name of Smith she married twice and twice was divorced from him.

Early in the nineties she moved to Blankenburg and settled down to a more quiet life in a house she owned in Uhlhorn avenue. As a reparation for some of her past misdeeds she resolved to have a church built in the neighborhood where she could attend services. Accordingly she donated a lot near the P.D.&E. railroad, $300 was scraped together in subscriptions and the building was started, but never completed. The unfinished [belfry], the rough steps, tell the story of ambitions bigger than pocket books. An unpaid lumber bill tells it even more eloquently.

When she deeded the property Mrs. Jones made the gift conditional that as soon as it ceased to be a General Baptist church the property should revert to her and if the building was not removed in a limited time it, too, should become her property.

Mrs. Jones became suspicious of church members, believing that they sought to cheat her out of the church. She was churched (disciplined) once on the charge of drinking and was expelled from the congregation.

Sister Jones was finally restored to good standing in the church, but the members of the congregation say she did not cease her scheming to get possession of the property. Last fall a revival was held. Soon a ghostly figure, all in white, began to appear during the evening services. It would peer in the windows, give hollow groans and show itself in front of the door as the people came out. It frightened the women and children and even the men did not dare to try to capture it but if the object was to scare the people so they would not hold services and the property would revert, it failed. It is said Mrs. Jones admitted to having been the ghost, dressed in her white skirts with a white spread thrown over her head.

Mrs. Jones was churched a second time on the charge of profane language. Again, she believed that this was an attempt to take the church property from her. Eventually, the congregation dwindled to fewer than twenty members, with even fewer attending weekly service. The moment church service stopped, Sister Jones planned on selling the building to satisfy debts.

Cowan, Delaware County

Muncie (IN) Morning News, July 17, 1895
THE COWAN GHOST
Discovered and Declared an Imposition
A Neat Scheme by Which Citizens Attempt to Flimflam an Aged Man, but It Did Not Work

Haunted houses in Delaware County are a scarcity. It has been a number of years since the county produced a real good ghost story. One of those kind that makes the listener lose his breath and his hair stand on end. It may be that natural gas does not agree with ghosts, but nevertheless the residents of Cowan, a village six miles south of Muncie, say that they have a haunted house.

All of the residents do not say that this house is haunted, and if the statements of several substantial citizens are to be relied upon these ghosts are very live ones and can talk the same as ordinary people.

Ten years ago, so the story goes, a well known woman cut her throat in a house in that town. The lifeless and bloody body was found by neighbors and they say that since that time the woman's ghost has paced the streets and alleys of Cowan. The house in which the horrible suicide occurred is now owned by an aged man, who rents the property and it is now occupied by a family who have become quite well acquainted with this ghost. During the night screeches and low moans can be heard about the premises and often a female appears at one of the windows. It is always ghastly white and is attired in white garments. The ghost does not tarry long but gives a few pitiful wails and bids farewell. The landlord has been having a hard time keeping the house rented as the renters are always told that the house is haunted and that this woman who cut her throat will be seen several times every week. But this story don't go any more as the ghost has been discovered and it is now known that it is an imposter.

Lately the owner of the property has been approached by several people who desired to buy the property. His price was a little high and now he has learned that the people who wanted to buy the property represent the ghosts thinking that by making the owner believe the house is haunted he will consent to sell the property at a nominal price. He is on to the scheme and now greets the ghost with a smile and has not yet reduced the price for the property. Should the work continue the News will be permitted to print an item about a real live ghost being filled with a buckshot or pierced by a bullet.

Deer Creek, Carroll County

Fort Wayne (IN) Sentinel, January 8, 1902

PLAYS GHOST TO GET RICHES

Mrs. Sarah A. Harkins, an aged widow of wealth, residing at Deer Creek, a small town nine miles northeast of this city [Flora], is the victim of unknown persons who are endeavoring through the instrumentality of ghostly visitations to get possession of her property. White figures are seen floating about her premises after nightfall and the uncanny noises which are produced frighten her so that she flees to neighbors every night for protection. On her return she always finds the furniture misplaced and a note of warning written in red ink. The strange shadows and weird sounds produced are attributed to a relative who hopes to frighten her into making a will.

College Pranksters Seeking Membership

Indianapolis, Marion County

Indianapolis (IN) News, December 6, 1900

They Chased the Ghosts

Brave Butler Girls Turned the Tables—Other Butler Affairs

Some of the young men at Butler College invented a scheme last night to frighten the young women at the college residence. The young men persuaded Mrs. J.D. Forest, the head of the residence, to chaperon a party consisting of the "dorm" girls and a number of young men, out toward an old cemetery north of Irvington, where two "preps" had been sent dressed up in sheets.

The excursion was great sport for the young students, who yelled and sang all along the route.

When the cemetery was reached, the merry students climbed the fence surrounding it, collected near some tombstones and began telling ghost stories. While one of the young men was relating an experience he had had with a ghost, two white figures were seen approaching from the north.

Instead of screaming and running away, as the young men expected them to do, the brave girls took after the white objects that were approaching. The two young men dressed up in the sheets feared that their identity might be discovered, and began to run from their pursuers. They had not gone far until they encountered a hedge fence, and the sheets were torn in shreds. The girls found out who the boys were, and now the laugh is on the would-be joke-players.

The article closes with another incident from Butler College. The night prior, some underclassmen failed to capture the sophomore flag from atop the college tower. There was a rumor that some freshmen and some "preps" would make a second attempt, but the sophomores would be ready and waiting.

Evansville, Vanderburgh County

Evansville (IN) Press, March 13, 1938

No Ghosts, Just College Pledges

Twenty-seven Evansville College students, Phi Zeta Fraternity pledges, Saturday night showed downtown Evansville what the well-dressed man is wearing—to bed.

They paraded thru the streets in night gowns which waved gracefully in the balmy breeze.

It was part of their initiation.

The event started at Sixth and Main Streets, where the ghost-like figures stood on the steps of the American Trust Bank and did things like reciting "Mary Had a Little Lamb," for the benefit of a large crowd of the curious.

Indianapolis, Marion County

Indianapolis (IN) Times, October 17, 1932
SCORES GATHER, BUT GHOST-GIRL FAILS TO SHOW
Cemetery Drives Cluttered with Motorists, All Seeking Phantom
Ghosting on Maple Road boulevard Saturday night proved a dismal failure to scores of persons who climaxed a week and numerous pay day parties by seeking Indianapolis' phantom.

Although warned of the falsity of the stories of an alluring feminine ghost, the boulevard and Northwestern avenue were cluttered with cars from shortly before midnight until after 3 Sunday morning.

The curious saw nothing and heard nothing except the clink of bottles in other cars. Some of the visitors to the land of ghosts were in such stages of jitters that they could have seen many things—including white phantoms—with but little stretch of the imagination.

MORE THAN 100 AT SCENE
Apparently; Miss Minnie Ghost doesn't cater to crowds. So far her only appearances have been before audiences of one and two.

Many of the Saturday night crowd at the northwest end of the cemetery halted their cars and settled down for a long wait. Others merely drove by, slowing long enough to make sure there were no ghosts in sight.

One man reported more than forty people at the scene, shortly after midnight; another said there were fifteen filled cars, while a third estimated the 2 to 3 a.m. gathering at more than 100 persons.

VERSIONS ALL SIMILAR
Miss Ghost swung into action more than a week ago and has had her activities related, with increasing gusto, until half the town is talking.

According to the story and its three versions, a young woman first appeared on a curb near the cemetery. A taxi driver started to take her to the address she gave. A few minutes later she disappeared from the cab and his investigation is supposed to have resulted in the information that the young woman, whose name and address he had, died three weeks ago.

Story No. 2 tells of two men on the boulevard at 2 a.m. a few nights later. They picked up the same pale and "half-dead" looking young woman.

No Trace of "Witnesses"

She told them the depression ended for her three weeks ago and then disappeared from the car. Their investigation also is supposed to have resulted in information that the girl has been dead three weeks.

And the third tale is that of a truck driver who is said to have had a similar experience except that the phantom, or whatever it is, rode with him from near the cemetery, disappeared en route to Thirtieth street and Capital avenue. He is supposed to have taken his wife to the address he had been given and learned—that the girl had been dead three weeks.

But there is no trace of the story tellers, the girl or phantom, or the address.

With overcast skies, who knows but what tonight may not be a typical ghost night?

Journal and Courier (Lafayette, IN), October 18, 1932

Unmasked Cemetery "Ghost" Proves to Be Frat Pledge

Several thousand motorists again risked all sorts of "supernatural" perils and gathered at the northwest edge of the big Crown Hill cemetery here [Indianapolis] early today hoping to be thrilled by a reappearance of the phantom girl with the flowing robe.

The crowd did get a thrill for the ghost—or was it another one?—suddenly popped into view.

Unfortunately for the ghost he popped into view from behind a telephone pole just as Mrs. Dolly Bramblett Kark, known as Mme. Bramblett, the spiritualist, was passing in her car.

While others started a grand exodus, Madame Bramblett quickly jumped from her car to hold conversation with the apparition. Like the phantom girl this ghost also extended a piece of paper toward the spiritualist. But Mrs. Kark wasn't interested in a scrap of paper. She moved toward the ghost with the apparent intention of laying hands on him.

Races with "Ghost"

The ghost wavered and then began to retreat. Mme. Bramblett increased her speed. So did the ghost. The apparition looked around, saw the spiritualist gaining. The race developed into a real chase.

Dr. Martin Luther King Jr. Street, then Northwestern Avenue, runs alongside Crown Hill Cemetery. This street, and others, would have been filled with cars and ghost hunters in October 1932. *Author photo.*

Believe it or not but Madame Bramblett in spite of her skirts overtook the ghost. She snatched the sheet from the figure.

No skeleton emerged from the sheet but a flushed, blond young giant. Seizing him by the wrist, Madame Bramblett demanded:

"Where are you going, ghost?"

"Lemme go!" whined the youth." "I ain't no ghost. I'm a fraternity pledge."

Youths Aid in Escape

By that time James McRae, his wife, Mary, and Mrs. Ruby Hall, friends of the madame, had surrounded the "ghost." But the ghost also had friends. About fifteen youths suddenly emerged from autos parked in nearby shadows and ran interference for the "ghost," who tore loose and fled.

Madame Bramblett lectured his friends about it being "serious business" to impersonate a ghost.

The opinion prevailed today that a Butler university fraternity had taken advantage of the phantom girl scare to put in a good initiation stunt. One local newspaper today put the fraternity "on the pan" for pulling the stunt.

Original investigators of the phantom girl apparition did not believe the "ghost" captured by the spiritualist this morning had any connection with the strange girl whose weird disappearing act is reporting to have put motorist into a hospital with a severe nervous shock.

Children Pranksters Creating Fun

Union City, Randolph County

Muncie (IN) Evening Press, July 14, 1936

Spook Story

Union City Has 13-Year-Old Ghost

East Side police were called Saturday night to arrest a ghost which residents in the neighborhood of Market and Main Sts. said was "haunting" them.

A.F. Medlam, East Side marshal, went to the rescue when two frightened citizens summoned him to the scene of the spook's activities.

The ghost was stalking up and down the street when the officer arrived, and neighbors kept a safe distance away.

Investigating, he found the ghost to be a 13-year-old girl, garbed in a white sheet.

Crown Point Cemetery in Kokomo, Indiana, was established in 1868. Visitors are welcome; lace curtains are optional. *Author photo.*

Kokomo, Howard County

Indianapolis (IN) Star, November 25, 1908
Play "Ghost" at Cemetery
Two Small Boys, Attired in Lace Curtains, Sent Home by Police
Roy Masters, 12 years old, and Lena Stout, 11, were intercepted by Patrolman Begrman at the gate of Crown Point Cemetery, where they were playing spooks, to the annoyance of pedestrians. They were attired in lace curtains and hiding behind the fence posts, extending their arms in spectral fashion. The patrolman sent them home.

Goshen, Elkhart County

South Bend (IN) Tribune, January 29, 1933
"Ghosts" Seized at Goshen Home
"Ghosts" which have been walking in the "haunted house" owned by Earl and Abe Neff, three miles and a half southeast of Goshen, walked into the hands of the law Tuesday night.

Neighboring farmers surrounding the vacant house Tuesday night and caught a total of 14 boys and girls, all local youths, who have been frequenting the place. Fathers of some of the young people have promised to pay about $300 damages done to the building and furnishings.

Morristown, Shelby County

Evening Republican (Columbus, IN), March 20, 1895
Exploits of a Ghost
It Is Robed in Black and Caused Great Excitement
Great excitement reigns in the south part of this place [Morristown] over the appearance of a ghost. Quite a number of ladies have been terribly frightened. Unlike the usual ghost, this one is clad in a long flowing black robe and veil. While Mrs. Jane Huffman and a niece were returning home from a neighbor's, this strange creature appeared in pursuit of them. Mrs. Huffman gave one scream and fell in a swoon. She still lies in precarious condition. A committee is forming to investigate the matter.

Indianapolis (IN) Journal, March 20, 1895
It is very wrong for that Morristown ghost to wear black, and so frighten people nearly to death. It ought to know that reform dress has not yet been adopted by members of its profession, and that white is still the rule.

Columbus (IN) Republican, March 23, 1895
The ghost mystery at Morristown has been solved. It was the prank of a roguish girl.

Near Warren

Fort Wayne (IN) Daily News, January 3, 1898
A real live ghost has been startling the citizens near Warren, Huntington county, Ind. It is white-sheeted and wears a Fedora hat, and haunts a bridge on the Montpelier road. Traffic across the bridge is suspended at nightfall.

Huntington (IN) Weekly Herald, January 7, 1898
Warren Has a Ghost
A hair-raising ghost story comes from Warren. The people there are much excited over the appearance of a ghost, which has been seen about two

miles east of Batson bridge on the Montpelier road. It is described as being a low, heavy-set figure, with black suit, white shirt and a light Fedora hat. It has made its appearance on a small culvert or bridge and when met by a person will always take the opposite side of the bridge and make an attempt to grab at the horses' head when accosted by any one driving along. It makes its appearance between the hours of nine and twelve o'clock each evening. During the last few evenings bobsled loads of curious people have visited the place armed for the mysterious thing, but as yet we have had no report from them. A party that visited the culvert Saturday night were not successful in seeing his ghostship.

Daily News-Democrat (Huntington, IN), January 14, 1898
The Spooks Exposed
People who see ghosts this day and age of the world, are either afflicted with the drink habit or else lack courage enough to feel safe after dark. It now transpires that the ghost seen down in Jackson township, near Baston's bridge, was nothing more nor less than four boys in the neighborhood who stood on the bridge on dark nights and frightened women as they drove along. Quite an excitement was worked up before the boys were caught at the trick.

Fort Wayne, Allen County

Fort Wayne (IN) Journal-Gazette, September 13, 1922
Fun-Loving Child Explains Mystery of Latest "Ghost"
The mystery of the "ghost" which has terrified the district about Gay street and Creighton avenue for the past several nights was solved last night by police officers. The object of fear of the entire community was found to be a little 14-year-old girl who, refused permission to play with the other little girls of her community, took the "ghost" act as a means of providing herself with amusement.

The child, dressed in pure white and flowing sheet, brought terror to the hearts of the other children of the community as well as to many of the older folks and it was not until she was finally located by the police that her fun was brought to a halt, much to the relief of the residents. Plain Clothes Officer Vashon located the child and after administering a severe lecture, took her to her home.

Evansville, Vanderburgh County

Evansville (IN) Courier, June 16, 1910
PANIC STRICKEN AT GHOST TRICK
Women and Children in Crowded Commencement Hall in Great Fright
A cry for help, coming from the darkness just outside the building where the graduation exercises were being held Wednesday evening at the Assumption Catholic church school hall, created a near panic, and in the rush of the women and children to reach the door several were bruised and a number of women fainted. Only the reassuring words of Father Eugene McBarron, who was addressing the graduating class, quieted the fears of the terror stricken audience and restored order.

The innocent pranks of a number of children who were playing "ghost" in the school yard was the cause of the excitement. One of the boys, with a sheet thrown over his head, passed through the light reflected through the window. The young son of Louis Herman, not "next" to the joke, saw the

The Assumption Catholic Church was sold to the city in the 1960s. The building was razed to make room for a civic center. *Courtesy of the Willard Public Library Archives.*

The school hall (not pictured) was built on the property of the Assumption Church. *Courtesy of the Willard Public Library Archives.*

apparition and cried for help. His appeal was [plainly] heard in the hall and fearing that it was a cry of fire, women and children made a mad scramble to reach the outside of the building.

After quiet had again been restored the program was resumed where it had been interrupted. Although the graduates were yet nervous from the excitement caused by the panic, they managed to carry on the program with credit to themselves and to the delightful entertainment of the large crowd of people who were in attendance....

Griffith, Lake County

Lake County Times (Hammond, IN), May 17. 1911
GHOST WALKS IN GRIFFITH
This town was considerably wrought up last night over the prank of a young lady, who put a white sheet over her head and meandered around the streets, frightening children. At the corner of Junction avenue and Main street a number of adults took to their heels when they saw the "ghost." A constable chased the young woman for a block and apprehended her. When he found the girl was "having fun," as she expressed it, he released her with a warning.

Some of our younger pranksters have earned the title of innovative pranksters, which appear in the next section.

INNOVATIVE PRANKSTERS

Jefferson County

Indianapolis (IN) News, January 9, 1886
THE GHOST OF BLOODY RUN[42]
A Blood-Curdling Mystery in Jefferson County Solved
The mystery of Bloody Run is solved at last, and the ghost and goblin yarns of that enchanted stream are but the offspring of imagination. He who would now harrow the superstitious soul with tales of goblin-gobbles and devil revels must find another spot for his goblins to gobble in, as Bloody Run has run its course as a witches' stamping ground. The following yarn, told by a farmer who lives on the border land of the haunted "diggins," will explain the mystery that has turned many heads gray and driven the gentle god of slumber from many superstitious souls:

A farmer, young in years but old in experience, killed a calf at a date deponent saith not, and filled the hide with hay and rags. When completed it presented a very fair appearance, and resembled in many respects the animal that once cantered around the farmer's barn lot. The ingenious youth was so pleased with his work that he tried his hand on an owl a neighbor had shot. With both these specimens of his handiwork in his possession, he was not long in concocting the scheme hundreds of people pronounced of supernatural origin. Bloody Run, surrounded as it was with the memories of robber bands and hidden wealth, was selected as a fitting place in which to operate. From a point several feet up the tree, at the foot of which the gold is said to have been buried, he ran a couple of heavy wires to the brow of the overhanging cliff. Through two rings he had placed on the back of the stuffed calf he passed one of the wires, and the other through the back of the owl. Fastening a rope to the calf and a light twine string to the owl, he was fixed. All that was necessary for him to do to make a ghostly calf or owl descend apparently from the clouds to that hole near the tree was to shove either over the bluff to slide down the wire. With the strings attached to each he could yank them back up the wires to his hiding place. Thus prepared he spread the first of the Bloody Run ghost stories, and let Mr. McLaughlin into the secret, who offered the $50 reward to any one who would spend the night at the foot of that tree in the hollow. The first man who undertook the job was armed with a shot-gun, a corn-knife and a base-ball bat. He sat three hours, but nothing appeared. At 12 o'clock a full blown calf came sailing through the air, with tail erect and singing like a telegraph wire. That was enough; the watcher wasn't looking for calves, as he hadn't lost any, and left on the double quick. The next man saw the biggest owl in America and struck out down the hollow over logs and through brush piles, just as the calf man had done the night before. For two weeks that farmer yanked that calf and owl up and down the wire, and so many had been the frightened watchers that had fled, a path was worn through the brush. A few nights ago the last of the watchers sat down at the foot of the tree and waited. The calf came down as usual, but alas! the wire parted and poor stuffed calfy struck poor Mr. watcher and knocked the wind out of him. He came to in ten minutes, and looked around to see where he was. There lay that confounded ghost, but the fall had "busted" its belly band and rags and hay hung out of it in three or four directions. Frightened no longer the man investigated, found the wire and the owl and "busted" the biggest ghost story of the season.

Petersburgh, Pike County

Princeton (IN) Clarion-News, June 15, 1926

Boys Hang "Dummy" to Scare Motorists

Small boys came near causing some prostrations on the state highway south of this city [Petersburg] late Sunday night when they hung a "dummy" to a limb on a nearby tree and awaited results. Most of the drivers put on speed when they saw the ghost and put as much distance between them and the spook as possible, but one driver investigated and stopped the boys' fun.

Nashville, Brown County

Brown County Democrat (Nashville, IN), March 3, 1921

"Not Afraid of Spooks"

But Mysterious Noises and a Creepy Feeling Cause Ed Snider a Sleepless Night

Ed Snider, a whole-souled and prominent citizen of Jackson township, has no fear of "spooks." He can read ghost stories hour after hour and then sleep without the least symptom of "night mare." He enjoys a hearty laugh when he hears some one tell of his experiences with a ghost.

A few nights ago Ed came to Nashville to spend the night with his son-in-law, Ivan Mobley at the home of Ivan's father Wm. Mobley. As he dozed off to slumber he was suddenly startled by a ringing noise above him. He listened attentively for some time, but no other sound. Perhaps 'twas just imagination! Having heard that "one dreams most when sleeping on his back" he turned on his side, and was soon in slumberland. Ting-a-ling! Ting-a-ling! Ed suddenly sat up. Ting, ting, ting-a-ling! His hair stood up, and his knees were nervous; he scratched his head and taxed his mental qualities to remember if any great crime had ever been committed in that particular house. Ting, ting! What the thunder? The room was dark. He lighted a lamp, and examined the walls and ceiling. Everything was as usual. From the adjoining room came the snoring of his son-in-law. Would he call him? No, not till the "thing" came back. It never did, but Ed never did sleep any that night. He rolled and tumbled in his bed, wondering if there really was such a thing as a spook.

Ivan and his wife had arranged a string from their bed up [through] the ceiling, then through to the adjoining room, and in the attic above Ed's bed the string was connected to a tiny bell. They kept Dad's "ghost" alive by pulling the string.

This was the second attempt of Ivan and his wife to work the spook trick, the first attempt being a miserable failure. The trick was originally planned for Ivan's brother, Rex, but Rex got next and when no one was around he attached the string to a bucket of water just above Ivan's bed. Ivan and his wife chuckled with glee when they heard Rex going to his room. Ivan pulled the string. "The blamed thing won't work," he whispered to his wife. "Maybe the string is caught," she said, "pull a little harder." He did! and about two gallons of ice cold water poured into their faces and all over the bed. As they were changing the bed clothing, etc., in an adjoining room an innocent young man was dreaming of the "old swimmin' hole."

Evansville, Vanderburgh County

Evansville (IN) Journal-News, November 24, 1914

Ingleside Develops Sure-'Nough Ghost

Ingleside, an addition near Howell.[43] has discovered a real ghost with the form of a dog and eyes and teeth of fire. The apparition is said to appear each night at 10 o'clock. Howell authorities were notified Tuesday and asked to "lay" for the ghost.

Mrs. Henry Tierman, living in the addition, first saw the specter. She was coming home from a friend's home Sunday night when it came down the road. She fled with cries into her home. Her husband, hearing her scream, met her at the door and fired two harmless shots at the unknown which proceeded down the road.

Miss Daisy Hurstman and her escort, Fred Jowl, of Howell, returning home from a show Sunday night, also saw the apparition. They are not able to describe it accurately. Howell officials said Tuesday that they would watch for it Tuesday night and see if solid shot would harm it.

Evansville (IN) Courier, December 12, 1914

They Find Ghosts and Spirit Bosses

Howell Night-Terror Discovered to Be Paper Scarecrow Operated by a String

All fears of a ghost which has haunted pedestrian traffic on a path between the Ingle coal mines and Barker avenue for the last two weeks were broken last night at 10 o'clock when Charles Friedley, 22 Bell avenue, and a fearless posse climbed down into the hollow where the ghost would start and dart towards passers-by and found that it was only a paper object. The strange figure of a ghost has been a mystery to Howell shop and other railroad employes, who would pass it after dark on their way home from work.

When Friedley and his gang descended into the hollow last night and grabbed hold of the paper scarecrow they heard two chaps in a clump of bushes some distance away, holding to a string, cry out, "Don't break up our man, we only want to scare some of those Howell girls who pass here." The youths then ran. It was found that the string which extended 100 feet away caused the object to make "spooky" motions when it was jerked.

English, Crawford County

Daily Republican (Seymour, IN), October 6, 1898
NOW A RAVING MANIAC
Peter Mackey, who was frightened a few days ago by an alleged ghost, is reported to be a raving maniac, with little hope of recovery. Mackey went to sleep in a house alleged to be haunted, and some practical jokers aroused him by hurling a white dog down the stairway near where he lay.

Carroll County

Noblesville (IN) Democrat, January 22, 1897
EYES LIKE FIRE
Over in [Carroll] county, about 10 miles from Logansport, the people are greatly excited over a ghost which is said to walk nightly along the shores of the Wild Cat creek. A party of folks returning from the church Wednesday night of last week, report that they were badly frightened by the ghost as it crossed the road and made for the timber along the edge of the creek.

The horses reared, plunged and snorted and it was with difficulty that they were kept from upsetting the wagon. The ghost is said to be a giant in size, taking steps 15 feet apart, and has hair on the head about three feet long, which flows around in the wind. Its eyes shine like coals of fire and loose flowing robes of white complete the picture.

One party started out armed with guns to kill or capture the monster, but failed to get near enough, though it was seen running through the creek bottoms.

Richmond (IN) Item, January 18, 1897
For a week or more residents along the Wild Cat pike, near the Carroll county line, have been tortured by a ghost. At a point in the road through a stretch of heavy timber a tall, white apparition suddenly confronts the people on the way to attend revival meetings, causing the wildest consternation. The ghost appeared to walk back and forth along the road, but when too closely approached went straight up in the air. An investigation developed that some boys had the figure of a woman suspended from a wire and pulley in the top of a tree. The figure was worked back and forth on a wire tramway or trolley, giving it the appearance of a woman of tremendous size walking up and down the road. During the day the figure was kept hidden in the top of a tree. The boys were working on a plan to provide the ghost with power of speech when discovered, using the wire and electrical instruments for the purpose of producing phonographic sounds.

Visitors might not see ghosts on Wildcat Creek, but they might find herons and people participating in recreational activities. *Author photo.*

Columbus, Bartholomew County

Muncie (IN) Morning Star, March 22, 1912

"Ghost" Frightens Women

Lads Hang Dummy on Telephone Wire to Scare Pedestrians

Women living in Franklin street were badly frightened on returning to their homes when what seemed to be a ghost suddenly swooped down on [them]. They screamed and ran for shelter. Some of the men, who saw the monster of the air, quickened their footsteps and did not stop to investigate.

The police were called. They found that a dummy had been dressed in men's clothing, a rope tied around the neck and the end thrown over a telephone wire. When any one passed, the boys lowered the dummy to make it appear that a man was hanging from the wire. The boys disappeared and the officers took charge of the ghost.

Monon, White County

Evening Journal (Monticello, IN), December 12, 1922

Monon Has Only Ghost in Activity

Appears Every Evening at Round House About Twelve P.X.

A real ghost has been in evidence at the round house for the past ten days to the night crews who kept the affair quiet till Wednesday night. The ghost appears in the midnight hours and is described as a white object, woman shape and size at first then becoming more [ethereal], growing to the height of 40 to 50 feet. Most of the performances are given on the cinders back of the round house. It is suspected that possibly a bloody murder has been committed somewhere near and that the place is haunted. In the meantime no cinders are being hauled. A posse was organized and on the scene Wednesday night, prepared to rout the visitor. The crowd waited and watched for the nocturnal visitor. After waiting till near midnight without results, the posse went home. Max Rogers, John Hale, Jim Simpson tarried, and 12:10 a.m. his ghostess appeared and after going through the usual gyrations faded away. The round house ghost is the talk of the town and a glance at him is being sought by many.

It has been tipped off to the [Monon] News that some tangible data will be secured that will disclose the identity of this night prowler in a short time. Everybody is invited to come to the round house and see this latest Monon thriller, to be observed only at night between the hours of 6 and 11:00 p.m.—when he walks.

Journal and Courier (Lafayette, IN), December 20, 1922

MONON GHOST SCARE FINALLY EXPLAINED BY NOVELTY DEALER

Practical jokers have been found responsible for the ghost hoax which for several weeks has terrorized the residents of Monon, Ind., through nightly appearances in the rear of the Monon round-house at the railroad junction. The explanation of a novelty dealer at Monon has solved the ghost mystery, and the excitement which for a while prevailed has practically died out.

The dealer claims that some unknown person regularly has been purchasing small toy balloons filled with hydro gas from him. The party also secured a piece of cheese cloth and draped it over the balloons, which at night gave the appearance of a woman's form rising slowly from the ground, ascending into the heavens and gradually disappearing from sight. It is believed that an invisible wire controlled the illusion.

North Manchester, Wabash County

Princeton (IN) Clarion-News, March 28, 1902

JUST THE WAY OF GHOSTS

An abandoned cemetery inside the city [North Manchester] limits was believed to be haunted, and many tales were told of a weird figure flitting across the grounds after the shades of night had fallen, sometimes accompanied by screeching noises. Finally the skeptical made bold to investigate, and it was found that mischievous boys had stretched wires across the grounds from fence to fence from which was suspended a woman's nightrobe. This was drawn back and forth by the little scamps, who howled with delight whenever frightened people took to their heels.

Greensburg, Decatur County

Journal and Courier (Lafayette, IN), June 16, 1922

GHOST SCARE IN GREENSBURG

Boyish Ingenuity Keeps Citizens in Terror Until Police Chief Exposes Trick

Greensburg citizens are recovering from one of the worst ghost scares in the history of this town, and their peace of mind is due to the initiative of Chief of Police Hugh Flint.

The scare occurred Wednesday night, when residents of North Franklin street were aroused about 9:30 by weird and terrifying noises coming from an abandoned house. The din kept up for more than an hour and a large crown gathered. Some of the more daring of the crowd approached the house and played searchlights through the house, but their fright was only increased when they could see no one within, or discover the source of the noise.

A call was put in to Chief of Police Flint. He entered the house and was greeted with a terrific outburst. He persevered, however, and soon discovered an excellent exhibition of boyish ingenuity. By an arrangement of string and wire, once a spectator opened the door, the doors were banged and pictures were released. Every article touched released another noise-making device.

The paraphernalia was removed to the extent that ghosts will not disturb residents further.

Columbus, Bartholomew County

Evening Republican (Columbus, IN), March 25, 1911
POLICE CATCH GHOST AND HAVE IT TO SHOW
People Who Do Not Believe in Ghosts Are Invited to Call at Police Headquarters and See It

People who do not believe in ghosts are respectfully invited to visit police headquarters and have their doubts scattered. There is a perfectly good doubt scatterer these in the shape of a ghost and Mr. Ghost was captured by the police Friday night at Thirteenth and Mechanic streets.

A call came for the officers from some one in that neighborhood and when the police responded they found a bunch of small boys busily engaged in being the supporting company for Mr. Ghost, who of course played the leading role. The ghost was tied to a telephone pole and was being jiggled up and down when people passed. The result up to the time the police were called had been assorted cases of hysterics to say nothing of the many years growth out of which several had been frightened.

The ghost was made of newspaper tied and pinned together until there was a body, arms, legs, feet, etc. The face was a mask which looked like a cloak model had been murdered and her head cut off.

The officers took charge of the ghost and returned it to police [headquarters] where it is now.

Waterloo, DeKalb County

Waterloo (IN) Press, January 9, 1902
A "GHOST" APPEARED
What Two Men Saw at the Cedar Creek Bridge
ALMOST SCARED TO DEATH
Some one bent on fun perpetrated what was intended for a joke at about eight o'clock Monday night. A representation of a woman, life size, made of paper, was attached by a rope on the Cedar creek bridge by the cemetery, and either so arranged that the wind moved it or otherwise some one held to the rope and manipulated it at the desired moment. About 8 o'clock, while it was very dark, Mr. Corrigan and Mr. Lewis Hatch were crossing the bridge in attending their duties at the long distance telephone test station, when the "ghost," without warning, walked out in front of Mr. Hatch, frightening him nearly to death. He screamed and was nearly thrown into the nervous prostration, and the next day kept his room at Hotel Locke, absolutely prostrated from the fright. Mr. Corrigan, when he saw the "apparition," immediately seized it and tore it down, and Mr. Hatch says that had it not been for Corrigan's action, he surely would have died from fright. Mr. Hatch is a stranger here having arrived only a few days ago from Maumee, Ohio, to relieve the employes in turn at the test station while they enjoy a short vacation. Such jokes are too frequently disastrous in results and ought not to be indulged in.

PRANKS WITH UNINTENDED CONSEQUENCES

Columbus, Bartholomew County

Evening Republican (Columbus, IN), October 11, 1904
A REAL GHOST STORY
Two Young Men Frightened Out of Their Wits Monday Night by Own Family
A "ghost story" comes from the eastern part of the city which came near ending seriously for two young men on whom the joke was played. According to the story the two young men had been in the habit of remaining out late and Monday night the people with whom they board decided to play a joke on them.

When the young men went home they were confronted by two ghosts which made uncanny movements on the front porch. The young men were startled at first and then as the ghosts grew more life like the awful horror of having a ghost about the house seized them. One of the young men fell down and lay prone upon the steps while the other ran as if his life depended on it. When the members of the family saw the boy on the porch they went to him and found his hands as cold as ice. He was in a bad way for awhile but was finally brought around. The other boy did not return home Monday night and was not seen until this morning. The names of the two young men are withheld by the family.

Huntington, Huntington County

Huntington (IN) Herald, September 23, 1919
GETS SHAKEN BY "GHOST"
OWNER OF RESIDENCE HAS ROCKS "TOSSED" AT HIM BY MAN
BOTH LOOKING FOR SPIRIT
Police Department Skeptical—Boys in Neighborhood Keep People Awake
On the square, do you believe in ghosts?

Monday evening the police department was besieged with calls and inquiries regarding the ghost said to be inhabiting the "hill."

Many varied and weird tales are coming from that part of the city. Boys claim that they see "it" here and there and then it disappears. One boy said that ghost appeared at their back door, and then disappeared.

Residents of that neighborhood are not nearly concerned about the pest as they are about the boys in that vicinity. Some of them claim that they were unable to get any sleep until after midnight Saturday night—not on account of the ghost, but on account of the noise the boy "hunters" made.

A call was sent in to the police department from Lafontaine street about 8 o'clock Monday evening. The voice said that they had "it" and asked that two patrolmen be sent up at once.

A hurried call was made by the department only to find that the parties had released the man they had "captured."

It seemed that the man who was living at 639 Lafontaine street had left the house by the rear door and gone around the house toward the street. As he came from the shadows, a man started throwing stones at him. The attacker was "taken in" and given a good shaking up, and told to await the police. The fellow begged off before the officers arrived, saying that he was returning home from work and thought that he had seen the ghost. That was why, he said, he started throwing stones.

An estimate of the men, women and children on the scene at the time the officers arrived was placed at between 200 and 300 persons. Many autos and motorcycles were packed along the curbing, while their owners were indulging in the favorite pastime sport—ghost hunting.

Indianapolis, Marion County

Indianapolis (IN) News, August 3, 1928

Ghost Stories, Playful Father, Screams; Police

Efforts of Fred Dyer, 1157 Villa avenue, to have a little fun with his children, caused police to make a run to his home Thursday night, they reported.

Dyer, the police said, had been telling ghost stories to the children, who finally became sleepy and retired. Then Dyer, the police said, climbed on the porch roof and playfully tossed a pillow through the window on to the children's bed. The screams that followed caused neighbors to call police.

Noblesville, Hamilton County

Indianapolis (IN) News, February 26, 1906

Coffin Peppered with Shot

James Parks narrowly escaped being shot to death Saturday night, while playing "ghost," to frighten his friend, Harry Simmerman. The latter is employed in a livery stable, and while asleep in a chair, some of his friends procured a coffin, placed it close to where the young man was sitting, while Parks, wrapping himself in a sheet, lay down in it. Some one in the crowd watching the developments from the sidewalk, called to Simmerman, and the first thing meeting his gaze, as he slowly opened his eyes, was the lid of the coffin slowly rising.

The second time the lid moved Simmerman seized a shotgun and emptied the contents of both barrels at the coffin. Parks quickly threw off the lid and jumped out, throwing aside the sheet and begging Simmerman to shoot no more. The sides of the coffin were perforated with shot, but Parks escaped unhurt.

Muncie, Delaware County

Indianapolis (IN) Morning Star, July 18, 1906
VICTIM OF STUDENT PRANK
Normal College Man Is Prostrated After Experience With "Ghosts"
Edward Gaunt, a young man whose home is in Portland, Ind., and who is attending Indiana Normal College here [Muncie], was unable to attend school today as the result of a prank which a few of his companions played on him Monday night. Young Gaunt had called on a lady and in returning to his rooming-house was accosted on the street by one of his classmates who was attired to resemble a ghost.

Bert Cunningham, who was in company with Gaunt and who knew of the joke, started to run. His companion became frightened and ran so swiftly that he fell, seriously injuring himself. During the night he was seized with prostration and a physician was called.

West Fork, Crawford County

Logansport (IN) Pharos, November 23, 1898
HALLOWEEN JOKE IS SERIOUS
Young Man Plays Ghost and His Sweetheart May Die as a Result
A practical joke on the eve of Halloween has assumed such a serious aspect that the victim's chances of recovery are very remote. Miss Evaline Dowden is an exceedingly popular and accomplished young woman of this place [West Fork], and her engagement to be married was announced for next month. With a number of friends she made arrangements to visit the cemetery at midnight, on the night mentioned, to enjoy the popular superstition of learning the future.[44] Her sweetheart heard of the girl's intentions and with two friends repaired to the graveyard in advance, dressed in white. They concealed themselves and when the young woman reached the spot sprung from their hiding places.

Miss Dowden, who was in advance, uttered a piercing shriek and turned and fled toward her companions, where she dropped in a swoon at the feet of the almost as badly frightened girls. The supposed ghosts ran to her assistance, calling out to reassure the girls, and all worked to restore her, only to see her fall into another swoon. Although temporary relief has been given these swoons have continued daily for three weeks, and it is feared now that it will cause her death. Grave fears are also entertained for her affianced, who is now suffering with brain fever.

Danville, Hendricks County

Mitchell (IN) Commercial, March 25, 1897
At Danville Harvey Walker played ghost and was fatally shot by a man whom he attempted to frighten.

Noblesville, Hamilton County

Noblesville (IN) Democrat, December 5, 1890
WORSE THAN ANTICIPATED
TWO PERSONS OF THE FEMALE SEX PLAY GHOST AND THE RESULT IS SERIOUS
About 8 o'clock last evening Mr. and Mrs. James F. Lauhon were at Craig's grocery near the Lake Erie depot purchasing the necessaries of life. It was when they were wending their way homeward on East Division street that James Lauhon [preceded] his wife about 50 feet, when they were within a square of their residence. Just as Mrs. Lauhon passed the alley that they are compelled to go by on their way home, two men came out therefrom, one making a remark to the other that they could see no ghost. Nothing was thought of the words by Mrs. Lauhon at the time they were made, so she reached her home unmolested.

Without removing her cloak she passed through the rooms and out upon the porch that is attached to the east side of the house. Just outside of the fence and about twenty-five feet from Mrs. Lauhon stood two forms clad in white with their arms [akimbo] making a low noise that they would attract her attention. Frightened almost to death Mrs. Lauhon uttered several screams and turned to run into the house when she came against the pump handle that was in a horizontal position and struck her breast a terrible blow. Dr. White the attending physician says that she may get along nicely if no further trouble sets in. The lady managed to get into the house but by what means she told a [*Democrat*] reporter this morning that she did not know. Mr. Lauhon had now procured a revolver and went out to investigate affairs and the two persons who are supposed to be ladies walked slowly slowly away and when about a square from the house they took off their white garments and joined the two men who are supposed to have been waiting there. Previous to this occurrence they entered the yard and presented their ghostly appearance at the window of Mrs. Anna Adams. These persons whoever they are should be run down and punished to the full extent of the law. 'Tis not a civilized country that will permit people to run at large [whose] sole object is to frighten and make other persons unhappy without any cause.

Somewhere in Indiana

Nashville (TN) Union and American, June 14, 1870

It is not very pleasant to play ghost in Indiana. A young chap recently attempted it on an old farmer, who believes in muscular Christianity, and the ghost had to be taken home in a wheelbarrow.

Marion, Grant County

Evening Herald (Huntington, IN), August 11, 1904

GHOST BREAKS HIS OWN NOSE

Apparition that Scared People Nightly Proves to Be a Young Practical Joker

A ghost has been frightening persons who live near Ohio and Sherman streets for several weeks, and no one has been brave enough to make a thorough investigation. The apparition always appeared at 9 p.m. as the curfew whistle sounded. Women and children in the neighborhood were frightened and before the hour arrived each night were within their homes.

Finally Harry Baker, 17 years old, was confronted by the white-clad figure as he walked along the street. Baker was badly frightened and started to run, the ghost pursuing him. The ghost ran against a tree, breaking his nose, and was rendered unconscious. When the flowing white robes were removed it was discovered that they covered the person of Oscar Demmick, a practical joker of the neighborhood.

NOTES

Introduction

1. Baldasty, *Commercialization of News*, 3.
2. Sachsman, "Introduction," xvii.
3. Sachsman, "Introduction," xviii.
4. Sachsman, "Introduction," xviii.
5. Sachsman, "Introduction," xviii.
6. Kilmer, "Haunted *Times*?," 106.
7. McGarry, *Ghosts of Futures Past*, 1.
8. Kilmer, interview.
9. Sachsman, "Introduction," xxiv.
10. Boswell, *Life of Samuel Johnson*.

Chapter 1

11. McDonald, *Lost Indianapolis*.
12. Mitchell, "RetroIndy."
13. "Real Spook Moans."
14. Mitchell, "RetroIndy."
15. To learn more about Riverside Amusement Park, see McDonald, *Lost Indianapolis*.
16. Great American Stations, "Elkhart, IN (EKH)."

17. Great American Stations, "Elkhart, IN (EKH)."
18. New York Central Railroad Company, "Greatest Highway in the World."
19. "Not Ghosts—Just Bull Frogs."
20. There is more than one Needmore in Indiana, the others being in Lawrence and Vermillion Counties. The dateline of the article states "Nashville, Ind.," so an educated guess would place this ghost story at the Needmore in Brown County. According to local legend, a storekeeper commented that the community *needed more*, so the name stuck.
21. Each Saturday, the *Richmond Palladium* offered a section just for children called "The Junior Palladium" (founded in 1916), where they were offered the opportunity to be reporters and contributors. Children were invited to submit their articles and questions for Aunt Polly in person by visiting the Palladium office (or via letter).
22. Tolleston is a former town and is now a neighborhood in Gary.
23. Indiana Harbor is located in East Chicago.

Chapter 2

24. Thornton, *Frankfort.*
25. Thornton, *Frankfort.*
26. "This House Is Haunted."
27. "A Haunted Schoolhouse."
28. The Independent Order of Odd Fellows (I.O.O.F.) is a fraternal order. Its mission is to "visit the sick, relieve the distressed, bury the dead and educate the orphan." This included establishing cemeteries in its communities.
29. What began in 1895 as a church bulletin, the *Indianapolis Recorder* (established in 1897) is one of the nation's oldest African American newspapers. The newspaper is still active today and can be found at https://indianapolisrecorder.com.
30. "Blind tiger" is slang for a place that sold alcohol illegally.
31. The American Society for Psychical Research was founded in 1885 with the mission "to explore extraordinary or as yet unexplained phenomena that have been called psychic or paranormal, and their implications for our understanding of consciousness, the universe and the nature of existence" ("About the Society").

32. The Aetna Powder Company was located in Aetna, Indiana, near Miller Beach, now both neighborhoods of Gary. Several fatal explosions at the Aetna Powder Company were found in the newspaper archives prior to this article's 1910 publication. Explosions resulting in deaths occurred in 1888 ("Blown Into Fragments"), 1890 ("Fatal Explosion"), 1891 (*Inter Ocean*, September 14, 1891), three in 1899 ("Explosion Kills Three," "Aetna Explosion Kills Four" and "Dynamite Explosion"), 1902 ("Second Powder Victim Dies"), 1903 ("Aetna Officals Insist"), 1905 ("Two Men and a House Blown Into Fragments"), 1907 ("Blown to Bits") and 1909 ("Blown to Atoms"). After the article was published, six lives were lost in the deadliest explosion at the Aetna Powder Company in 1912 ("Six Are Killed"). The explosions caused earthquake-like shocks felt for miles.
33. Dubbed the "Everglades of the North," the Grand Kankakee Marsh "meandered from the area that would in time become South Bend across the northwest corner of Indiana and into Illinois" ("A Look Back"). The marsh was once one of the largest wetlands in North America (500,000 acres), attracting many hunters due to its robust wildlife (Jasper County Public Library). Beginning around 1854, the wetlands began to be drained for agricultural and economic expansion. The wetlands were home to a large wolf population, which developed an almost mythic status as they became feared by neighboring communities (Taylor, "Call of the Wild").
34. Alex's last name is used twice in the article and spelled differently each time, so no educated guesses were made on the correct spelling and kept as is.

Chapter 3

35. Harter, *Fort Wayne*, 56.
36. "Joker Causes Ghost Scare."
37. "Police Aided in Perpetrating Ghost Hoax."
38. "Ghost of Hope Hospital," Lyric Theatre advertisement.
39. Webb, "Evansville Ghost Story."
40. The article ends with "THE BIG FOUR TODAY" and lists who they married and where they settled.
41. The initials are from the contributor of the story. The story was included in a series called "One Exciting Night." As stated, "Two dollars

is paid for every article printed under the heading, and additional special prizes, ranging from $10 to $50, are to be given for the best ones." I wonder if H.G. received a special prize for his spooky story?

42. Bloody Run was a stream that flowed into the Indian Kentuck Creek in Jefferson County, Indiana.
43. Howell is a neighborhood in Evansville, originally serving as a railroad town annexed by Evansville in 1916.
44. Originating from the British Isles, it was once a popular American tradition to foretell futures and summon future spouses at Halloween through a variety of rituals, including divination with food, mirrors, water, fire and so on.

BIBLIOGRAPHY

"Aetna Explosion Killed Four." *Wilkes-Barre (PA) Times*, October 13, 1899.

"Aetna Officials Insist Only One Man Was Killed." *Indianapolis (IN) Morning Star*, November 27, 1903.

American Society for Psychical Research Inc. "About the Society." http://www.aspr.com.

Baldasty, Gerald J. *The Commercialization of News in the Nineteenth Century*. University of Wisconsin Press, 1992.

"Blown Into Fragments." *Chicago (IL) Tribune*, April 7, 1888.

"Blown to Atoms." *Los Angeles (CA) Times*, August 14, 1909.

"Blown to Bits by Explosion." *Lake County Times* (Hammond, IN), April 2, 1907.

Boswell, James. *The Life of Samuel Johnson*. Project Gutenberg, 2013. Originally published in 1791. https://www.gutenberg.org.

"Dynamite Explosion Kills Two." *Fort Wayne (IN) News*, November 4, 1899.

Earlham Cemetery Inc. "About Earlham Cemetery." http://earlhamcemetery.com/about-earlham-cemetery.

East Hill Cemetery Company of Rushville. "History of East Hill Cemetery." http://easthillcemetery.com.

"Explosion Kills Three." *Daily Inter Ocean* (Chicago, IL), May 23, 1899.

"Fatal Explosion at a Powder-Mill." *Daily Journal* (Logansport, IN), December 17, 1890.

"Five Employes Blown to Atoms." *Champaign (IL) Daily News*, November 26, 1903.

"The Ghost of Hope Hospital." Advertisement for the Lyric Theatre, *Fort Wayne Daily News*, September 10, 1917, 6.

"'Ghost of Old Hope Hospital' Captured, Photographed, Cautioned and Discharged." *Fort Wayne (IN) Journal-Gazette*, September 6, 1917.

Great American Stations. "Elkhart, IN (EKH)." https://www.greatamericanstations.com.

Harter, Randolph L. *Fort Wayne*. Postcard History series. Arcadia Publishing, 2013.

"A Haunted Schoolhouse." *Indianapolis (IN) News*, June 27, 1902.

Historic Evansville. "Assumption Catholic Church." https://historicevansville.com.

Indiana Memory. "American Steel and Wire Co., Anderson, Indiana." https://digital.library.in.gov.

Inter Ocean (Chicago, IL), September 14, 1891.

Indiana State Board of Health Monthly Bulletin 25, no. 10. Photo of J.N. Hurty (n.d.): 126. https://hdl.handle.net/1805/8451.

Jasper County Public Library. "Local History in Your Library: Dredging of the Kanakee River and the Grand Kankakee Marsh." https://www.myjcpl.org.

"Joker Causes Ghost Scare." *Fort Wayne (IN) Daily News*, September 5, 1917.

Kilmer, Paulette D. "Haunted *Times*? Ghosts in Crime Stories Printed by the *New York Times*, 1850–1901." In *After the War: The Press in a Changing America, 1865–1900*. Edited by David B. Sachsman. Transaction Publishers, 2017.

Kilmer, Paulette. "Finding Ghosts in Newspapers." Interview by Teri Finneman. *Journalism History Podcast*, October 27, 2020. https://journalism-history.org.

Library of Congress. "Wayne County Courthouse." http://www.loc.gov.

"A Look Back: Kankakee Marsh Was Largest Inland Wetlands in U.S." *South Bend (IN) Tribune*, April 9, 2018.

McDonald, John P. *Lost Indianapolis*. Images of America series. Arcadia Publishing, 2002.

McGarry, Molly. *Ghosts of Futures Past: Spiritualism and the Cultural Politics of Nineteenth Century America*. University of California Press, 2008.

McMaken, Corey. "June 23, 1961: Demolishing Interior of Lyric Theater." *Journal-Gazette*, June 6, 2022. https://www.journalgazette.net.

Mitchell, Dawn. "RetroIndy: Riverside Amusement Park, The Summer Resort Within City Limits." *IndyStar* (Indianapolis, IN), July 23, 2019.

New York Central Railroad Company. "The Greatest Highway in the World: Historical, Industrial and Descriptive Information of the Towns, Cities and Country Passed Through Between New York and Chicago via the New York Central Lines, c. 1921." Project Gutenberg, 2009. Retrieved from https://www.gutenberg.org.

"Not Ghosts—Just Bull Frogs." *Mitchell (IN) Tribune*, May 23, 1929.

"Police Aided in Perpetrating Ghost Hoax." *Fort Wayne (IN) News*, September 6, 1917.

Purdue University Archives and Special Collection. John N. Hurty Papers. https://archives.lib.purdue.edu.

"Real Spook Moans in 'Haunted House,' but Ghost Is Laid." *Indianapolis (IN) Sunday Star*, August 30, 1936.

Sachsman, David B. "Introduction." In *After the War: The Press in a Changing America, 1865–1900*. Edited by David B. Sachsman. Transaction Publishers, 2017.

"Second Powder Victims Dies." *Inter Ocean* (Chicago, IL), October 3, 1902.

"Six Are Killed; Score Injured." *Indianapolis (IN) Star*, November 13, 1912.

Taylor, Stephen J. "The Call of the Wild: Bounties, Taxes, & Terror." *Hoosier State Chronicles*, September 1, 2015. https://blog.newspapers.library.in.gov.

"This House Is Haunted." *Decatur (IN) Democrat*, December 21, 1894.

Thornton, Janis, and the Clinton County Historical Society. *Frankfort*. Images of America series. Arcadia Publishing, 2013.

"Two Men and a House Blown Into Fragments." *Courier-Journal* (Louisville, KY), October 3, 1905.

Waynet Inc. "Wayne County, Indiana's Courthouse." https://www.waynet.org.

Webb, Jon. "Evansville Ghost Story Ended with a Wrongly Accused Man Getting Released from Prison." *Evansville (IN) Courier and Press*, October 31, 2023.

Willard Public Library Archives, Evansville, IN. Photos of Assumption Church. https://www.willardlib.org/archive-services.

ABOUT THE AUTHOR

Ashley Watson received her PhD in rhetoric from Purdue University, her master's from Miami University of Ohio and her bachelor's from Purdue. She writes about haunted history, commonplace books and spooky folklore on her blog NotebookofGhosts.com. In addition, she maintains a newspaper archive of ghost stories proven to be false (sometimes humorously so) at ItWasNotaGhost.com. Ashley shares her passions of photographing cemeteries, making zines, collecting ghosts and Halloween decorations and reading spooky short stories on her popular Instagram account @notebookofghosts. Ashley lives in West Lafayette, Indiana, with her husband, James; her stepson, Hollis; and their dogs and cats.

Visit us at
www.historypress.com